D0998347

WITHDRAWN
UTSA LIBRARIES

Early Book Illustration in Spain

Flos sanctorum.

La vida de nŕo señoz iesu cristo:

z de su sctíssima madre: z ỏlos otros scỏs: segũ la ozdẻ de sus fiestas.

Pedro de la Vega. *Flos Sanctorum.* Zaragoza, G. Coci, *c.* 1521

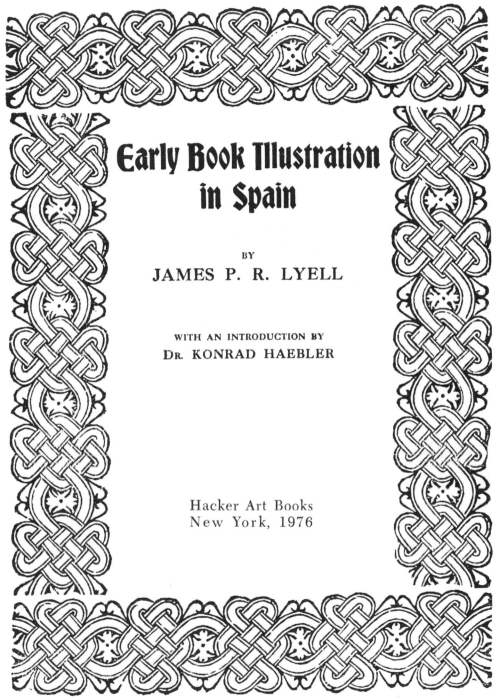

Early Book Illustration in Spain

BY

JAMES P. R. LYELL

WITH AN INTRODUCTION BY

DR. KONRAD HAEBLER

Hacker Art Books
New York, 1976

(From *Historia y Milagros de nuestra Señora de Montserrat*, 1550)

First published 1926 in London
Reissued 1976 by
Hacker Art Books, New York

Library of Congress Catalogue Card Number 70-143357
ISBN 0-87817-076-6

Printed in the United States of America.

LIBRARY
The University of Texas
At San Antonio

EGREGIO · DOCTORI · CONRADO · HAEBLER

PIETATIS · ERGO

HOC · OPUSCULUM

MAGISTRO · DISCIPULUS

D. D. D.

PREFACE.

As far as I am aware, no book has ever been written in any language dealing with the special subject of early book decoration and illustration in Spain in the fifteenth and sixteenth centuries.

The attempt made in these pages, to give a brief outline of the subject, suffers from all the disadvantages and limitations which are associated with pioneer work of this kind. I am fully conscious of the inadequate qualifications I possess for any critical and technical study of early woodcuts, and can therefore only crave the indulgence of experts, while respectfully venturing to hope that a perusal of these pages may lead some recognised authority on the art of the early woodcutter to turn his attention to a branch of the subject which hitherto has been neglected in a manner, at once remarkable and much to be regretted. For many years I have been interested in early printing in Spain, and nobody who has handled the early printed books, which contain woodcuts produced in the Peninsula during the last quarter of the fifteenth, and during the first half of the succeeding century, can fail to be impressed with the abundance of interesting material that deserves adequate examination and discriminating consideration. For this reason, I am hopeful that the large number of facsimile reproductions which illustrate my text, may reveal to some who have not hitherto recognised it, the interest, and often the considerable artistic merit, which are to be found in the early illustrated books printed in Spain.

In the pages that follow, I have first of all dealt with the illustrated books which appeared during the first decade of the existence of the printing press in Spain. I have followed this with an outline of the work at each important town until the end of the fifteenth century. Where the work of individual printers has overlapped into the sixteenth century, it has been treated, for the purposes of convenience, in this first part, a portion of which formed a paper on the subject, which I had the honour of reading last year to my fellow-members of the Bibliographical Society.

The work in the sixteenth century, dealt with in the second part, has been limited, almost entirely, to those printers whose work was confined to that century.

Bibliographical references will be found, as a rule, in the footnotes, the chief exception to this rule being the *Bibliografía Ibérica del Siglo XV.* of Dr. Konrad Haebler (in two parts, Leipzig, 1903-1917), which is cited throughout under his surname, followed by the particular number of the entry in his book. Every attempt has been made to provide a comprehensive and useful Index.

Spanish early printed books have always been scarce, and of recent years have become difficult, if not almost impossible to obtain. Some of them apparently only survive in single copies, while of many only two or three copies are recorded. It is perhaps unnecessary, therefore, to select for special mention any particular books among those dealt with in the following pages. However, attention may be directed to the remarkable illustrations appearing in the Zamora edition of *Los trabajos de Hercules* in 1483 (pp. 8-15), to the interesting series of the fifteenth-century Indulgences, and particularly to the discovery of a variant issue of the one printed in Toledo in 1484, while in the next century, one printed in 1504 in connexion with the pilgrims visiting Santiago de Compostella, has more than mere typographical or decorative interest (pp. 6, 7, 17, 89 and 283).   The fine work of Juan Rosembach at Barcelona, and the history of his 1522 edition of St. Bonaventura's *Vita Christi* (p. 50), deserve notice.   The *Flos Sanctorum* of Pedro de la Vega, printed by Coci at Zaragoza, *c.* 1521 (p. 129), is one of the most striking examples of the early picture book, and affords, as far as I am aware, the earliest example in Spain of colour printing in so many colours, the style and workmanship of which can be seen in the frontispiece to this volume, where a portion of the title-page has been reproduced.   Among books which, apart from their illustration or decoration, have historical or literary interest, will be found a contemporary discussion on the validity of the divorce of Queen Catherine of Aragon by Henry VIII. (p. 189), the Spanish story at the time of the Armada, as it sailed from Lisbon in 1588 (p. 305), the Spanish original of the first work printed in England on the science of navigation (p. 212), and several works dealing with the discovery of the New World, including the Spanish *Marco Polo* of 1529.   In addition, there will be found early illustrated medical and astronomical books, early comedies from the Spanish stage, illustrated romances of chivalry, for which Spain in the sixteenth century was so famous, and the first book published by her great dramatist, Lope de Vega.

I have not hesitated, whenever I have considered it to be of interest and appropriate, to deal with the authors and contents of some of the books which have come under review, and even of the association interest of some of the particular copies from which reproductions have been made.   I realise that this may outrage the feelings of some bibliographical purists, but to me, a bibliography is only a means to an end, and that end, the acquisition of all possible information concerning the literature of the country in which the books were produced.   A mere catalogue of titles and woodcuts would not, in my opinion, do full justice to the subject, and for my part, it is as much an absurdity to catalogue a fifteenth-century tract with a precise collation, and at the same time omit to mention that it contains the first, or one of the first, references to the discovery of America, as it would be to somewhat overload a book of special bibliographical, or technical interest, with a superfluous amount of biographical or literary information.   My task has to some extent been simplified by the possession of a moderately representative collection of early Spanish books, more especially of those printed in the sixteenth century.   Above all, it has been rendered possible by the generous advice and assistance I have received from friends, both in this country, Spain and elsewhere.   To the authorities of our own National Library, in common with all students, I am under deep obligation.   My indebtedness to Sr. Don Edouard Toda and Sr. Don P. Font y Rubinat, distinguished Catalan bibliographers, for help and assistance freely given, deserves, as it receives, my grateful acknowledgment.

Dr. Konrad Haebler, of Dresden, the admitted master on the subject of the early Spanish printing press, has assisted me with his advice and opinion on more than one debatable point. For his great kindness in reading the proofs and in writing an introductory note to my book, I am also much indebted.   In conclusion, my thanks are due to Messrs. Maggs Bros., Messrs. J. & J. Leighton, Ltd., Mr. W. Voynich, and, very specially, to Sr. Don R. Miquel y Planas for the loan of the blocks from which a few of the reproductions have been made, in the cases where I have not had the books themselves available for the purpose. My readers will also no doubt share my appreciation of the manner in which Messrs. Emery Walker, Ltd., have reproduced the coloured frontispiece, as well as the manner in which Mr. R. B. Fleming has taken the photographs from which a large majority of the illustrations has been reproduced.

J. P. R. L.

Savage Club, Adelphi,
London, *February*, 1926.

CONTENTS.

LIST OF ILLUSTRATIONS.

(Except where otherwise stated, all the illustrations have been taken from copies in the collection of the author.)

INTRODUCTION.

AMONG the books printed during the fifteenth century those issued from Spanish presses are the scarcest of all. The National Library in Madrid owns indeed the largest number of Spanish incunabula, but even its collection is very far from being complete. It may be that the collections of early printed Catalan books in Barcelona are nearer to completeness than are those of Madrid in respect to Spain as a whole. But Barcelona still lacks a considerable part of the Catalan production. Besides, Spanish incunabula are dispersed throughout the world. There are a few unique copies in the National Library at Paris, some more in the British Museum and other English collections. Some very fine specimens have gone to American libraries. But unique copies of Spanish early printed books are also to be found in the University Library of Upsala and in the State Library of Berlin, and even such an out-of-the-way institution as the Municipal Library of Breslau boasts of a Salamanca book apparently printed in the fifteenth century of which no other copy is known. It is rather a difficult matter, therefore, to make a comprehensive study of early Spanish printing. I think this is the reason why Spanish students in recent times have abstained from writing comprehensive works about the matter. Spanish students are not great travellers. In the eighteenth century the foundations were laid of the study of early printing in Spain. The works of Caballero and of Mendez are still the indispensable bases of any serious study of Spanish incunabula. Moreover, Spanish students have contributed since then some very valuable monographs on

printing in single places. What Serrano y Morales has done for
Valencia, Sanchez for Zaragoza, Jiménez Catalán for Lérida, Arco
for Tarragona, is of the utmost value for the study of early
Spanish printing. But the comprehensive works of recent times
are rather due to non-Spanish authors. Mr. Lyell is one of
these. He has had uncommonly fine opportunities for the study
of Spanish books of the fifteenth and sixteenth centuries. He
has visited Spain, and has not only made a thorough study of
the treasures assembled in the principal Spanish libraries, but,
moreover, he has been able to get together a considerable
collection of rare Spanish books, among which, although the
sixteenth century is largely represented, there are, in addition,
some precious and scarcely known Spanish incunabula and
some other items, which, although they are of the beginning
of the sixteenth century, have a considerable value for the
study of their early printed predecessors. Mr. Lyell draws
attention to a fourth book adorned with the fine woodcut
border that contains the name of Nicolas Spindeler and was
used first in the famous edition of *Tirant lo blanch*, issued by
this printer in 1490. We know that it passed afterwards to
the hands of Johann Rosembach, who probably was a companion of Spindeler in Valencia, but went on shortly afterwards
to Barcelona, where, with short interruptions, he practised
almost for forty years. I am of opinion that the newly discovered book (see Fig. 15) is another production of Rosembach's press; his are the types, and the border is used in the
same way as it was in the two editions of the *Constitucions* of
1494 issued by Rosembach. On the other hand, Mr. Lyell
reveals to us that borders passed in a similar way from the
press of Rosembach to that of Spindeler. I have elsewhere
directed attention to a border which has been used by Rosembach and by Luschner in several missals and in some other

books, in a very curious manner. This border has been cut
to pieces, and these were used in various ways as the size of
the books, where they are found, demanded it. Two pieces
of this border, that principally intended for the top and that
for the foot of the page, have been used in 1506 by Nicolas
Spindeler in a *Commentum in psalmos* of Jaime Perez de
Valencia (Fig. 16), where the foot piece is used as left-hand
border, the top piece being again used as the top, but in an
inverted position. And even this is not all that this title-page
has to tell us. For at the base of it, there is to be found
another border which, too, is not an unknown one to the
student of early Spanish printing. It is the representation of
the Arms of the Spanish Kings, which for the first time is to
be found in the edition of the *Constitucions* of 1493, issued
by another printer of Barcelona, Pere Miquel.

These incidents prove a fact commented upon by Mr.
Lyell in quite a number of other cases, viz., the transference
of woodcut materials from the hands of one printer to another.
I am not, I must confess, a competent judge of Spanish printing of the sixteenth century, which is treated in the second
division of Mr. Lyell's book. As in other countries, sixteenth-
century printing in Spain is much less known than that of the
previous century. There is only one monograph of scientific
importance by Sr. Sanchez on Zaragoza. What else we know
of it was founded almost entirely on the Salvá-Heredia Catalogues and in the Bibliografía Gráfica of Sr. Vindel. But
these were mere catalogues without any attempt at scientific
treatment. Perhaps Mr. Lyell's studies in sixteenth-century
illustrated books of Spanish origin cannot be said to be the
last word on the matter. But more than in the first division,
the subject has been dealt with from the sources to be found
in Mr. Lyell's own collection, and we are given a surprisingly

excellent estimate of the importance of this collection by what he has been able to show us in text and plates. His researches confirm, what we knew before, that book illustration in Spain had almost reached a maximum height at the end of the fifteenth century, and that it maintained its quality during the first decades of the next one. But from 1550 onwards it began to decline, and the specimens produced towards the end of the sixteenth century do not present any scientific importance. The same thing is seen in other countries as well. In the case of Spain there is, moreover, another point that contributes to the result. It seems that metal cutting and copper plate have been used in Spanish printed books earlier and oftener than they have in other countries. At the end of the sixteenth century and throughout the seventeenth, copper plates have more or less monopolised the title-pages of Spanish books. It is far from being always good work, but it is a new and a rather individual method of book illustration wholly different from what it had been before. So the end of the sixteenth century is an appropriate terminus for the study of the subject in Mr. Lyell's work, and he is to be congratulated upon resisting the temptation to go beyond that date. He has given us for the first time a comprehensive view of Spanish book illustration from the beginnings up to the time when a change of materials brought with it a change of style, the ramifications of which are not to be studied merely in book illustration or decoration. His researches are especially valuable in regard to the sixteenth century, where he has been more or less a pioneer in a field which has been scarcely explored. In such circumstances, it is not possible to make an exhaustive study of the subject. But, "In magnis voluisse sat est. Vivat sequens."

KONRAD HAEBLER.

PART I.

THE FIFTEENTH CENTURY.

CHAPTER I.

EARLY DAYS.

THERE are two examples of xylography in the Print-Room of the British Museum of the early part of the fifteenth century, which on account of their having been discovered in Spain, are, in default of any definite proof, assumed to be of Spanish provenance.

These are two "dotted prints." One of them represents the Mass of St. Gregory, with symbols of the Evangelists, while the other one depicts the Trinity, with St. Peter and St. Paul and two angels.

These two prints were formerly pasted in the binding of a book, said to have been imported from Spain from Huesca, where they had been discovered in an old printing office, from which woodcuts and fragments of wood blocks had also been obtained.

With the exception of these two prints, there are no early Spanish woodcuts in the Print-Room of the British Museum.

Little or no trace can be found in Spain, before the introduction of printing with movable types, of any general circulation of wood engravings, which would correspond with those, mainly of religious subjects, which were crude, highly coloured, and formed part of the education of the people of Germany and Holland during the first half of the fifteenth century and even later. Up to the present, I know of no Spanish block books of the school of the *Ars moriendi*. No dated *St. Christopher* by any unknown

Spanish master ! On the other hand, my experience teaches me that it is the unexpected that always happens in the way of fresh discoveries about the early history of Spanish arts and crafts, and therefore it would be foolish to be at all dogmatic upon the point. That this is so, is evidenced by the progress that has been made in investigating the history of wood and metal engravings, prior to the invention of printing, in Catalonia. For example, in an article "L'Art del Gravat a Cataluñya en els segles XV and XVI," which has recently appeared in *Bibliofilia*, a review published in Barcelona, which deals with the early typography and bibliography of the Peninsula, but principally confined to Catalonia, it is quite clear that there were xylographic prints in the form of religious representations, in Catalonia, during the first half of the fifteenth century. Mention is made of the discovery by Mossén Josep Gudiol, the curator of the Diocesan Museum at Vich,[1] in what I take to be a register of the inventories of personal property of deceased persons, of entries which relate to prints of various religious subjects. For example, in 1403, a certain Francesch Manya, of Vich, had a print on paper of the Crucifixion. In 1420, Joan de Noguer, " barber de Vich," had one of the Virgin and Child and St. Gabriel ; while in 1428, a notarial record has been found of Bishop Jordí D'Ornos instituting a priest to the church of Sant Esteve de Granollers, who when he took possession of the Rectory (" casa rectoral ") on the 16th of June of the same year, found " algunes cedulas de contractas stampades." It is obvious, therefore, that to some extent at least, xylographic printing preceded ordinary printing in the Peninsula, but surviving examples are extremely few, although there are several specimens of the work of Barcelona playing-card makers, from 1442 to 1468, extant in the Museum of Vich and elsewhere. Moreover, a reproduction of a primitive *taille-douce* metal engraving of the Prince of Viana,

[1] Vich, an ancient Spanish town, 40 miles north of Barcelona, with a cathedral dating back to the fourteenth century.

circa 1462, will be found reproduced in *Bibliofilia* (vol. II, p. 106).

The introduction of printing into Spain was later than in most of the other large European countries, although it was established at least three years earlier than in England.

The first Spanish printed book has been attributed to Lamberto Palmart at Valencia in the year 1474.[1] Palmart was probably of Flemish origin, and he, and most of the very early printers in Spain, were either Germans or Flemings. As a result we find that the cuts in Spanish fifteenth-century books were at first taken mainly from blocks brought into the country from Germany and other countries, or were copies made from the cuts in books which had already appeared in other parts of Europe. The output of illustrated books in Spain in the fifteenth century, though only small in itself, is fairly high in proportion to the total output of the press. Of 900 (or thereabouts) Spanish incunabula now known to exist, about 200 possess one or more woodcuts. In England the proportion is less than a tenth.

As far as I can trace, the first dated book with illustrations printed in Spain appeared in 1480. This was an edition of the *Fasciculus temporum* of Werner Rolewinck, an abridged history of the world, which found readers in many countries, from its first appearance in Cologne in 1474 until as late as 1532. Many editions were published, and among them one of the rarest is the Spanish edition, printed at Seville in 1480, by Alonso del Puerto and Bartolomé Segura.[2]

A comparison of this Spanish edition with the one printed by Georg Walch, a German, at Venice in 1479, shows clearly the source from which it derived its inspiration. In the setting of the pages, practically identical (except that the Spanish edition

[1] Recent investigation suggests the possibility that Palmart had other associates, all of them working under the direction of a master of the name of Jakob Vizland. (See Konrad Haebler, *Geschichte des spanischen Frühdruckes in Stammbäumen*, Leipzig, 1924.)

[2] Hain, 6927 (not seen) ; Haebler, 583 ; Brit. Mus. (I.B., 52305).

has seven extra leaves at the end devoted to the lives and customs of the philosophers), and in the imitation of the cuts, there is abundant evidence that Puerto and Segura worked with a copy of Walch's edition before them.

¶Turris babel.

FIG. I.—*Fasciculus temporum*, Seville, Puerto y Segura, 1480.

The cuts consist of concentric circles, interspersed with outline cuts, representing biblical scenes and characters, with the usual views of cities, such as Rome, Venice, etc., which we are accustomed to find in early books of this class. The Tower of Babel (Fig. 1), and the representation of the City of Rome

(Fig. 2) will at once be recognised by those acquainted with the earlier editions of the work.

Before leaving this particular Seville press, attention may be called to the *Bula de indulgencias en favor de la christianisacion de Guinea* (Fig. 3), which comes from the same press, and has a well-executed woodcut seal, besides exhibiting a type of unusual character. My example, printed upon vellum (Haebler, 111, (6)), was at one time in the possession of Ludwig Rosenthal, of Munich, and is the only recorded copy. Rosenthal placed it

FIG. 2.—*Fasciculus temporum*, Seville, Puerto y Segura, 1480.

c. 1477, while Haebler considers it to be of the same year (1480) as the *Fasciculus temporum*. I incline to think it was issued shortly after the *Repertorium* of Montalvo, printed by Martinez, Puerto y Segura in 1477. An initial letter M in the Bull is the same as used in the *Repertorium*, and I cannot trace it elsewhere. The Vatican authorities, with whom I have been in communication, can give no assistance in fixing the actual date of the issue of this Indulgence.

At Zaragoza in 1481 there appeared a *Psalterium cum canticis*, produced by an anonymous printer whose types are found subsequently in the possession of Pablo Hurus and Enrique Botel.

The first page of the text has a striking xylographic capital B in the opening word of Psalm 1 ; this represents King David with his harp. These same printers also printed an *Arte de bien morir*

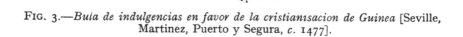

FIG. 3.—*Bula de indulgencias en favor de la cristianisacion de Guinea* [Seville, Martinez, Puerto y Segura, *c.* 1477].

about the same time, with cuts of obviously German character and origin. Under 1481 we may also mention a *Bula de indulgencias en favor de la iglesia de San Salvador de Avila*, printed in the monastery of Nuestra Señora del Prado in Valladolid,[1] which is not only the first recorded piece of printing at that town but has a clearly designed woodcut seal and some other slight decoration. Haebler describes it as "esta preciosa bula," and it is here reproduced from the only recorded copy (Fig. 4).

Up to the present, we have not been able to mention any book in which both the author and the illustrations can, with

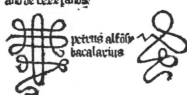

FIG. 4.—*Bula de indulgencias en favor de la iglesia de S. Salvador de Avila* [Valladolid, en el monasterio de Nuestra señora del Prado, 1481].

any reasonable certainty, be described as wholly Spanish. The first work which at all answers to such a description is *Los trabajos de Hercules*, of Enrique de Villena, printed at Zamora, by Antonio de Centenera, on the 15th of January, 1483.

Villena was of royal descent, on his Father's side, from the royal House of Aragon, and on his Mother's side, from the Kings

---

[1] Haebler, *Bibliografía Ibérica*, III (2).

of Castile.   Born in 1384, he died in Madrid in 1434.   In an age that was wild and rude, he acquired a literary reputation, which in more civilised times, it might be a little difficult to understand.   Juan de Mena and the Marquis de Santillana, in the old cancioneros,[1] have sung his praises, the former describing him as " honrra de España y del siglo presente."   This is not the place to discuss the truth of such contemporary eulogies, but in introducing to your notice the first illustrated book of any importance in the Spanish language, some particulars of the author are at once necessary and appropriate.   Although originally intended for the Army, Villena speedily forsook arms for letters, and devoted himself to his literary studies, with an application and assiduity extremely rare among those of his own social standing, the large majority of whom at the time could neither read nor write.   Under these circumstances, it is not difficult to understand why he was accused of sorcery, or why, after his death, his library was submitted to Friar Lope de Barrientos, a Dominican, who was Confessor to King John II., who ordered some 100 volumes to be burned.   His literary works which have survived, consist of a treatise on the art of poetry ; a curious book on the art of carving, which might be described as an epicure's guide to the pleasures of a royal table ; besides translations of Dante and the *Æneid*, and this translation into Spanish of the *Labours of Hercules*.   It is a book which Ticknor, in one of his expansive moments, has described as " one of the rarest books in the world," and which Latassa, in his well-known bibliography of Aragonese writers,[2] most unaccountably omits altogether.   It commences with a letter of the author addressed to a Catalan friend, Pedro Pardo, at whose suggestion he narrates the deeds and valour of Hercules.

There are twelve chapters in the book, each containing one

---

[1] Juan de Mena, *l as Trescientas*, Seville, 1499 (copla cxxvii), and the *Cancionero General*, Toledo, 1527 (fol. xviii).

[2] Felix de Latassa, *Diccionario Bibliografico-Biografico*, Zaragoza, 1884.

FIG. 5.—Villena *Los trabajos de Hercules*, Zamora, Antonio de Centenera, 1483.

FIG. 6.—Villena—*Los trabajos de Hercules*, Zamora, Antonio de Centenera, 1483.

of the labours.   These are discussed under four heads : (*a*) " Hys-
toria nuda," or the commonly accepted version of the incident,
(*b*) the " Declaraçion," or explanation of the allegory, (*c*) the
" Verdad," or the historical facts capable of being cited in support
of the story, and (*d*) the " Aplicaçion," or moral to be drawn from
it.   In this analysis, he reduces the human race into twelve states,
or conditions, namely : Princes, Prelates, Knights, Members of
Christian Religious Orders, Citizens, Shopkeepers, Labourers,
Mechanics, Teachers in the learned professions, and last, but by
no means least, Women !

The book abounds in references to classical authors, e.g.
Lucan, Ovid, and Virgil, very uninteresting to modern readers,
but fresh and novel to the Spaniards of the time in a rendering in
their own language.

Before we proceed to discuss the illustrations, a word may
be said as to the press.   Antonio de Centenera commenced work
at Zamora in 1482.   Unlike some of his contemporaries, he was
very economical in the information disclosed in his colophons.
For example, in this book he merely states that these labours of
Hercules were completed at Zamora, on Wednesday, 15th of
January, the year of our Lord, 1483, and this is followed by his
surname, " Centenera," a lack of advertisement, which argues, as
was the fact, an absence of any competing press in the town.
There are eleven cuts in the book, of an average measurement of
141 × 96 mm., each occupying nearly one-half of a full page.
From the reproductions given, it will be seen that these are apparently metal cuts, and that the work is striking, if archaic.   It
is unlike anything else I have come across of this period, and
there is not very much doubt that we have here the work of a
native Spanish artist.

The first reproduction (Fig. 5), which is the fourth cut in
the book, shows Hercules with the well-known monster Cerberus.
The second (Fig. 6), the fifth cut in the book, represents the
capture of the mares of Diomedes.   In this cut, attention may

be called to the black and white tiled pavement, which, with the
general grouping of the figures, gives it a more finished appearance
than any of its predecessors.

The third reproduction (Fig. 7), being the sixth cut in the
book, shows Hercules after his fight against the Lernean Hydra.

xliij

ella vſaua de nueuas fuerças z mas
dañoſos enpeſçimientos. en tãto que
los babitantes de aquella region no
podian ſobzelenar tanto embargo ní

nos auer alguno eſpaçio para mozar
z tozrnar en o ala patría o mozaða
o tierra ſuya. Ala qual la natura z
natural amoz mucbo los ínclínaua.

FIG. 7.—Villena—*Los trabajos de Hercules*, Zamora, Antonio de Centenera, 1483.

The fourth (Fig. 8), the eighth cut in the book, depicts him
killing the great Antæus, a son of Neptune, one of his lesser-
known exploits. It was after this incident that, proceeding on
his journey, he erected two pillars on the two sides of the Straits
of Gibraltar, thereafter known as the " Pillars of Hercules." The

fifth reproduction (Fig. 9), the tenth to appear in the book, shows another of his adventures which is not usually included among the twelve labours.   He is shown engaged in killing a

℃ Eſtado de maeſtro.
     I noueno trabajo de ber
cules fue quando lucho
con ātheo el gigāte ⁊ lo
vencio ⁊ mato.
     ℃ Hyſtoria nuda.
℃ Eſta byſtoria ba en ſus libros pu

los ombres ocupando con violencia
la ſeñoria de libia. Eſte deſuſaua de
los mas continuos puertos los mer
cadores ⁊ mareantes no auiendo lle
na ſeguridad ni podiendo del confiar
que muchas vezes ⁊ a muchos la fe
⁊ ſegurāça falleſcido auia Ceſaua por

FIG. 8.—Villena—*Los trabajos de Hercules*, Zamora, Antonio de Centenera, 1483.

giant hog which he had encountered among the Calydonian mountains, the resort of the Arcadian Atalante, who is introduced into the story.

The last reproduction (Fig. 10), and also the last in the book, depicts Hercules supporting the heavens as *locum tenens* for Atlas, an incident in his search for the golden apples of Hesperides, which leads our author to describe it as one worthy to be included among the other good deeds which he did in the world.

The other five cuts in the book deal with the fight with the Nemean lion, the Stymphalian birds, the golden apples of

FIG. 9.—Villena—*Los trabajos de Hercules*, Zamora, Antonio de Centenera, 1483.

Hesperides, the Cretan bull, and the fabulous robber, Cacus, who had stolen his cattle.

For the period this is a very remarkable book, and both the text and the cuts deserve more attention than they have hitherto received. One point of interest arises in connection with the work of the printer. A glance at the cuts will show that they were separately printed after the text, as in several instances the cuts over-run the letterpress through careless press-work. I do not recall another instance of this in any other fifteenth-century Spanish book of this particular period, and as

ⅭⅩⅤⅡ

Ⓒ Eſtado de muger.
l dozeno trabajo de ber
cules fue quãdo ſoſtuuo
el çielo conlos ⁊ enſus õ
bzos en lugar de atalan
te que tal cargo le enco
Ⓒ Hyſtozia nuda.

ta de ſu reyno ⁊ puſoſe ã ſoſtener cõ
ſus õbzos el çielo. maguer le fueſe ex
celſiuo trabajo eſtuuo ocupado eñſta
cura faſta eſperar remedio que poz a
yuda de otro mas valiente fue proue
ydo al ſoſtenimiento del çielo ⁊ confir
maçion de aquel. Ⓔ quãto duro la ſu

FIG. 10.—Villena—*Los trabajos de Hercules*, Zamora, Antonio de Centenera, 1483.

far as other countries are concerned, Dr. Ernst Crous, of Berlin, whose knowledge of incunabula during the last few years has been very special, tells me that similar instances are rare, and that in this matter there is no distinction between cuts on metal or on

wood.   I recall, however, that some of the ornamental borders
of Ratdolt at Venice are found overlapping the text on the title-
page, indicating that they were printed after it.

The recorded copies of this book are in the Grenville
Library of the British Museum, the Biblioteca Nacional at
Madrid, the Library of the Escorial, a British Museum duplicate (the Salvá copy), sold during the war and now in America,
and the copy in the writer's possession.

Fig. 11.—Villena—*Los trabajos de Hercules*, Burgos, Juan de Burgos, 1499.

A second edition of this book was produced by Juan de
Burgos at Burgos in 1499, with an entirely different set of
cuts, which Professor A. W. Pollard has adequately described as
" poor illustrations " (Fig. 11).

Our survey of illustrated or decorated books during the first
decade of the printing press in Spain may be concluded by draw-
ing attention to a very early, if not the earliest, example of the
art in the city of Toledo.

Pérez Pastor, in his bibliography of Toledo,[1] reproduces in facsimile a Papal Bull of Indulgence, issued by Sixtus IV. in connection with the war against the Moors.   This was printed by Juan Vasquez at Toledo, and Pastor describes it as the first piece of printing in that town.   He attributes it to the year 1483, but Haebler in his *Bibliografía Ibérica* (No. 94) clearly shows, by internal and other evidence, that the correct date is 1484, Pastor having probably misread a manuscript date inserted in his copy.   A single quarto sheet printed on vellum, it consists of forty-three lines of type with two small cuts.   One of these comprises two figures and the two opening words of the document, all within an oblong border.   The other cut, in the shape of a circular seal, represents the Virgin and Child.

I have recently acquired another copy of this Indulgence, also printed upon vellum, but with variations which, up to the present, have been unrecorded.   The cuts and the type are identical, and with one exception the text is the same, but instead of forty-three lines there only thirty-nine in my copy, more of the words having been abbreviated (Fig. 12).

There is one interesting difference in the text.   In my example the amount of the offering as an acknowledgment of the indulgence which was granted is supplied in manuscript in the space left blank for the purpose, with the words, " dos florines," while in the Pastor copy the sum is printed as " seys reales de plata Castellanos."   Apparently this latter was the sum usually expected, but it was found convenient not to have a fixed tariff in some cases, and thus in some examples the space was left in blank.   The date written in my copy is May 1484, and this particular indulgence had been granted to the Condesa de Oropesa, a member of a well-known family among the Spanish nobility, the first Count being Fernando Álvarez de Toledo, whose creation dates back to some twenty years before the date of this

---

[1] Cristóbal Pérez Pastor, *La Imprenta en Toledo*, Madrid, 1887.

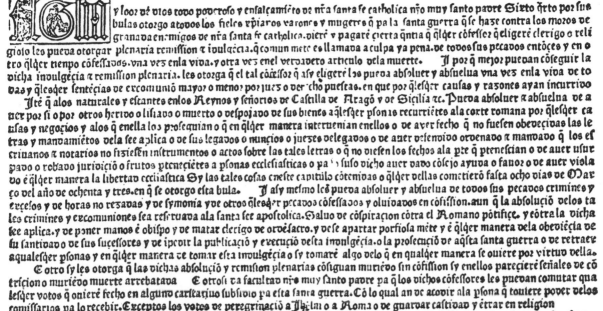

FIG. 12.—*Bula de indulgencias de la Santa Cruzada* [Toledo, Juan Vasquez, 1484].

indulgence. The priority in date of printing between these two copies cannot be determined with any degree of certainty, but they hold the field at present as the earliest productions from any Toledo press.

Pending further discoveries it would seem that book illustration, or even book decoration, did not amount to very much in Spain during the early years of the printing press in that country. Native craftsmen had been few, and the new art had no doubt been faced with the passive indifference which characterises the attitude of the Spaniard to anything novel and unusual. On the other hand, the Spanish people, always individualistic in their tastes and habits, very soon impressed a distinctly Spanish tone and character upon their printed books. The foreign printers who settled in the country speedily assimilated the Spanish atmosphere. It has always been so, and nothing has struck me more than the rapid manner in which foreigners, who come to reside in Spain, are drawn into the life and habits of the people. I have come across little colonies of Scotsmen engaged in the exportation of Esparto grass for British paper manufacturers, or in supervising the technical work of a copper mine, all of whom, by intermarriage and the special force of their environment, have become almost as Spanish as their native neighbours. It was thus, that being accustomed to the bold characters in their manuscripts, the Spaniards never took kindly to Roman type, and this in spite of the fact that their earliest books were printed with it. Gothic type very soon became almost universal, and it was usually specially rich and round in its design.

In the pages that follow, as we proceed from town to town, and observe the development of the decoration and illustration of their books during the concluding years of the fifteenth century, and where the printers overlap, during the opening years of the succeeding one, we shall see, and be able to appreciate, the very special characteristics of early Spanish books which have given them a place, and a very distinctive one, in the history of early typography in Europe.

FIG. 13.—*Tirant lo Blanch*, Valencia, Nicolás Spindeler, 1490. (Reduced.)

FIG. 14.—*Constitucions fets per D. Fernando*, Barcelona, Juan Rosembach, May, 1494.

CHAPTER II.

THE ILLUSTRATED BOOKS AT VALENCIA AND ZARAGOZA.

WE will commence our survey with Valencia, the birth-place of Spanish printing. Among the books of Palmart, the first printer, with one trifling exception, I can find none with illustrations. We must turn, therefore, to Nicolás Spindeler, one of the peripatetic printers of German origin, who came originally from Saxony, and printed most of his books at Valencia, although he also worked from time to time at Tortosa, Barcelona, and Tarragona. He is responsible for, perhaps, the most beautiful printed page in any Spanish fifteenth-century book, the well-known recto of the first leaf of the text of *Tirant lo Blanch*, which he printed in 1490 (Fig. 13). There are three existing copies of the book, an imperfect one in the University Library of Valencia, one in the collection of the Hispanic Society of America, and the specially fine copy in the Grenville collection in the British Museum. It is of interest to note that the copy in America is without the fine border to the first leaf, and it is clear that there were two distinct issues of the book.[1]

Tirant lo Blanch has not only the distinction of containing one of the best pieces of book decoration in any fifteenth-century Spanish book, but it is also the first known romance of chivalry printed in that country. Martorell, the author, has given the work a distinctly English flavour and shows a good deal of knowledge of English habits and customs. A large part

[1] *Vide* J. Ribelles Comín, *Bibliografía de la Lengua Valenciana* (pp. 393-410).

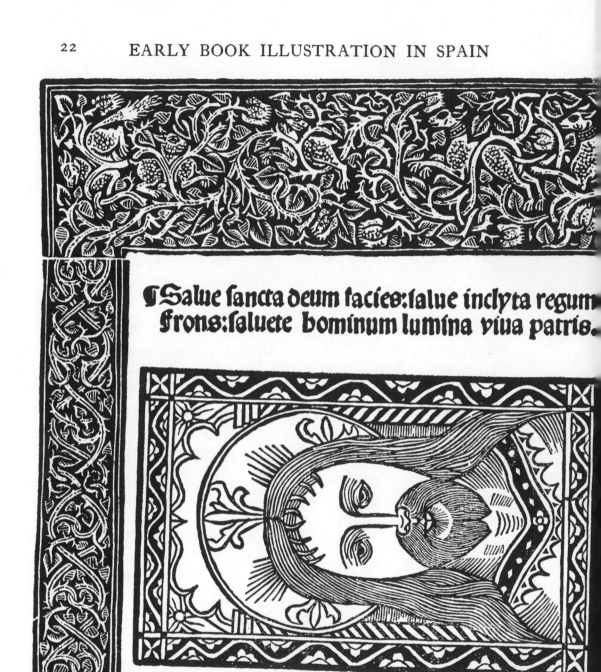

¶Salue sancta deum facies:salue inclyta regum
frons:saluete hominum lumina viua patris.

¶Laus tibi fundator:tibi laus reserator olympi:
Quem tuleras nobis laus tibi virgo parens.

FIG. 15.—Nebrissensis—*Gramática*, Barcelona, Juan Rosembach, *c.* 1500.

of the book is based on the story of *Guy of Warwick*. This is not the place to pursue the literary contents of the book, which will be found adequately dealt with by Dr. Henry Thomas in his indispensable work on these Spanish romances of chivalry.[1] The wonderful border which appears in *Tirant lo Blanch*, was used by Juan Rosembach in his *Constitucions fets per D. Fernando* (Haebler, 168), which he printed in May, 1494 (Fig. 14). I have recently found it again at Barcelona in a grammar of Nebrissensis, *c.* 1500, an edition unrecorded by Haebler, but which he tells me was, in his opinion, also printed by Rosembach (Fig. 15).

Another of Spindeler's books must be mentioned, the *Omelia sobre lo psalm del Miserere* of Vinyoles, printed in 1499, of which the only known copy is in the University Library at Valencia. On the verso of the title it has a fine and striking full-page cut, representing David on his knees in front of an army, his helmet and harp on the ground, and the Almighty pictured among the clouds in the act of blessing him. In the background there is a hill surmounted by a castle, with a view of the sea and a large ship. In this book the cut has no border, but I have found the cut again seven years later in a *Commentum in Psalmos*, by J. Pérez de Valencia, also printed by Spindeler, but at Barcelona (Fig. 16). The impression of the cut in 1506 is excellent, and it is now within borders, two of which, the lower and outside ones, are of considerable merit. This particular edition of Pérez de Valencia's commentary is, like the Vinyoles, only known in one copy, and its acquisition has enabled me to settle definitely the fact that such an edition existed, a fact doubted by Serrano in his dictionary of Valencian printers.[2]

Lope de Roca printed in Valencia from 1495 to 1497. The suggestion that he printed a single book in the city in 1485 being now generally thought to be groundless. In 1497,

---

[1] Dr. H. Thomas, *Spanish and Portuguese Romances of Chivalry*, Cambridge, 1920.
[2] Serrano y Morales, *Diccionario de impresores Valencianos*, Valencia, 1898-99 (p. 536).

FIG. 16.—Vinyoles—*Omelia sobre lo psalm Miserere*, Valencia, Nicolás Spindeler, 1499.

Also,

J. Perez de Valencia—*Commentum in psalmos*, Barcelona, Nicolás Spindeler, 1506.
(With borders.)

he produced two books with cuts, the *Vita Christi*, of Isabel de Villena, which is notable for his simple and well-designed device,[1] and *Lo Proces de les Olives y Somni de Ioan Ioan*, of Fenollar, reproductions of the illustrations in this book being reproduced in *Bibliofilia*, the excellent Catalan Review, published by Sr. Don Miquel y Planas, who spares neither time nor money to place on record the typographical rarities of Catalonia.

Diego Gumiel, one of the most decorative printers of the time, cannot be omitted when the illustrated books of Valencia are under review. Although his fifteenth-century work was confined to Barcelona he subsequently removed to Valladolid, and from there to Valencia, where he continued to print until 1517. His two Valencian books which call for special notice are the *Ars inventiva veritatis* of Ramon Lull, and the *Aureum opus regalium privilegiorum civitatis et regni Valentiae*, both printed in the year 1515.

The *Ars inventiva* has a fine title-page printed in red and black, and within a decorative border, in the lower compartment of which two somewhat uncomfortable-looking figures are holding up a blank shield, evidently designed for the owner of the book to insert his armorial bearings. The arms of Cardinal Ximenes de Cisneros, Spain's famous statesman, ecclesiastic, soldier, and man of letters, to whom the book is dedicated, occupy most of the page. On the verso of the second leaf there is a cut which represents the mountain of Randa, situated near Palma, in the island of Mallorca, which will ever be famous as the birthplace of the author, Ramon Lull, whose philosophical writings and erudition, far in advance of the thirteenth century in which he lived, earned him the title of " Doctor illuminatus." One of the most remarkable thinkers of medieval times, he was at once a great Spanish philosopher, the founder of Spanish mysticism, and a religious teacher, who, taking his life in his

---

[1] Serrano y Morales, *Diccionario de impresores Valencianos*, Valencia, 1898-99 (p. 502).

FIG. 17.—Lull—*Ars inventiva veritatis*, Valencia, Diego Gumiel, 1515.

hands, was one of the pioneers in missionary enterprise, while in his *Blanquerna* he found time to write a very remarkable Christian romance of chivalry. The most striking cut in the *Ars inventiva* appears on the verso of fol. 100, and depicts the martyrdom of Lull at Bujía [1] (Fig. 17). This cut presents the peculiarity that the title label at the top was originally cut with the town as "Tunis." In my copy there has been a cancel slip printed, in the same type and contemporary with the book,[2] with the correct name, "Bugia," and this has been pasted over the word "Tunis." The British Museum copy has the block in its first state, and if it ever had the cancel slip, it has come away. Some fine initial letters and the singularly beautiful device of Gumiel contribute to make this book an example of really artistic early printing.

The *Aureum Opus*, with its outline woodcut borders and its imposing heraldic title-page, is one of Gumiel's most successful efforts. The large equestrian cut of King Jaime illustrates nearly all the methods employed by the early woodcutter (Fig. 18). For example, we have here shading by parallel lines placed closely together, of uniform and unequal length. We have white dots on a black ground, cross hatching and small alternate black and white triangles. In the book there is also a large initial letter, cut on metal, with portraits of Ferdinand and Isabella, which we first find in a *Copilacion de leyes*, printed by Alvaro de Castro at Huete in 1485.

Pedro Trincher, who printed two books in this town in 1498, had one of them illustrated, viz.: the *Obra A Llaors de Sant Cristofol* (Haebler, 487), which has a fine cut on the verso of the title, which represents the Saint, with the Infant Christ in his arms, walking on the waves and being worshipped by two onlookers (Fig. 19).

---

[1] The modern Bougie, a port of Algeria on the coast of Africa.

[2] The copy is in another respect in contemporary condition, having its original limp vellum binding with string ties. It was formerly in the Heredia, William Morris, and George Dunn collections.

FIG. 18.—*Aureum opus*, Valencia, Diego Gumiel, 1515.

Zaragoza was the second town in which printing took place in Spain. Mateo Flandro printed a copy of the *Manipulus*

FIG. 19.—*Obra A Llaors de Sant Cristofol*, Valencia, Pedro Trincher, 1498.

curatorum there in 1475. While it is not illustrated, it has the distinction of being the first book printed in Spain, in which both the name of the printer and the place of printing are given. We have already mentioned two of the early Zaragoza books, which contained cuts and which were the work of an anonymous printer in 1481 (see pp. 5 and 6).

Attention may be called to a group of books which were produced there during the last ten or eleven years of the century, all of which are profusely illustrated, and many of the cuts in

FIG. 20.—Rodrigo de Zamora, *Spejo de la vida humana*, Zaragoza, P. Hurus, 1491.

which, if not actually printed from the same blocks, are exceedingly close copies of previous German editions of the same works. They came from the press of Pablo and Juan Hurus. These men were Germans, and had come to Spain from Constance, a city which at that time had intimate commercial relations with the east of Spain. It is not, therefore, difficult to understand the reasons which actuated these men in establishing a printing press at Zaragoza. Of the books included in this group, we may take as outstanding examples, the *Aesop* of 1489, the *Spejo de la vida humana* of Rodericus Zamorensis, printed in 1491, the

Mujeres ilustres of Boccaccio (1494), the *Defensorium inviolatae virginitatis Mariae* (*c.* 1495), and the *Breidenbach* (1498).

The *Aesop* of 1489 was produced by Juan Hurus, and has over 200 cuts, the only surviving copy being in the Library of the Escorial. Sánchez[1] has reproduced the large full-page woodcut portrait of Aesop, and also one of the cuts from the

FIG. 21.—Boccaccio—*Mujeres ilustres*, Zaragoza, Pablo Hurus, 1494.

text, and from these it is at once apparent that the cuts were copied from the edition produced by Sorg at Augsburg in 1486, who in turn had been indebted to an edition printed by Zainer at Ulm as far back as 1477.

The *Spejo de la vida humana* of Rodericus Zamorensis contains thirty-nine fine cuts, one of which is here reproduced (Fig. 20). The cuts are taken from the Augsburg edition of Zainer in

[1] J. M. Sánchez, *Bibliografía Zaragozana del siglo XV* (No. 17).

1476, and subsequently the same cuts appeared in the Lyons edition of the *Miroir de la vie humaine* in 1482, printed by Philippe and Reinhart.

The *Mujeres ilustres* of Boccaccio, for which Pablo Hurus was responsible in 1494, contains some seventy-five well-designed cuts. The book deals with notable women, from Eve onwards, and the selection presents a wonderful catholicity of taste. You will see the story of Pyramus and Thisbe introduced by Shakespeare

Fig. 22.—Boccaccio—*Mujeres ilustres*, Zaragoza, Pablo Hurus, 1494.

in his *Midsummer Night's Dream* (Fig. 21), Anthony and Cleopatra (Fig. 22), an alleged incident in the life of Pope Joan (Fig. 23), and the suicide of Seneca in his bath (Fig. 24).

All of these cuts are taken from the actual blocks used by Sorg in his edition of the same book at Augsburg in 1479, he himself having laid under contribution an edition printed by Zainer at Ulm in 1473.

The *Defensorium inviolatae virginitatis Mariae* is an extraordinary production, which for a long time was not recognised as a product of this press.   It has sixteen leaves printed on one side of the paper only, and each leaf has four cuts with descriptive letterpress underneath each cut (Fig. 25).   The first two leaves have only two cuts each and the fifth leaf has three cuts, making a grand total of fifty-nine cuts in all.   The only known copy of the book is in the Bibliothèque Nationale in Paris.   A block book to all outward appearance, it was for long considered to be one, until the Gothic type of the letterpress was identified as that used by Pablo and Juan Hurus for titles and chapter headings.[1]

This was discovered about 1910, when W. L. Schreiber, the authority on German woodcuts, published a facsimile reproduction.   The author of the book was Franciscus de Retza, and it first appeared as a block book by Friderich Walthern, at Basel in 1470, and it is from this block book, or another one in 1471, printed by Johann Eysenhut, that this Spanish typographical edition has, more or less, been faithfully copied.   Haebler ascribes the printing to Pablo Hurus, c. 1495, as in that year he had printed the *Triumfo de Maria*, in many respects a companion volume and also containing similar cuts.

We now come to the *Viaje de la tierra sancta* of Bernardo de Breidenbach.   The book was produced " a costas y expensas de Paulo Hurus aleman de Constācia " 16th January, 1498.   This famous and pioneer illustrated book of travel of the fifteenth century has been the subject of a special monograph[2] by Mr. Hugh W. Davies, a bibliographer, whose excellent catalogues of the early German and French books which belonged to the late Mr. C. Fairfax Murray are monuments of painstaking and original research.

Bernhard von Breydenbach was Dean of Mainz, and

[1] A facsimile reproduction of this book was published by W. L. Schreiber in 1910.   *Defensorium inviolatae virginitatis Mariae aus der Druckerei der Hurus in Saragossa in Faksimile-Reproduktion herausgegeben von Wilhelm Ludwig Schreiber*, Weimar, Gesellschaft der Bibliophilen, 1910.

[2] H. W. Davies, *Bernhard von Breydenbach and his Journey to the Holy Land*, 1483-4, London, 1911.

FIG. 23.—Boccaccio—*Mujeres ilustres*, Zaragoza, Pablo Hurus, 1494.

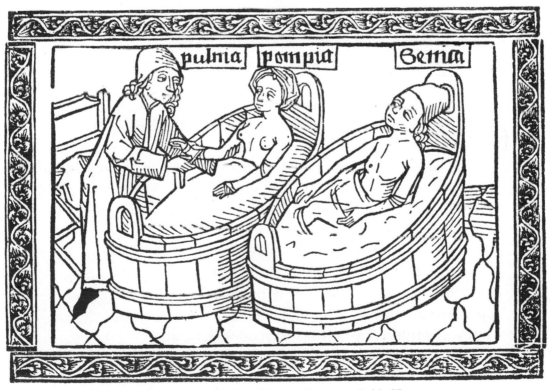

FIG. 24.—Boccaccio—*Mujeres ilustres*, Zaragoza, Pablo Hurus, 1494.

he was accompanied on this tour by a party of friends.   They
started from Venice, and some of them returned home after they
had reached Jerusalem, while the remainder went on to Mount
Sinai, returning to Venice via Alexandria.   It is difficult to
realise, in these days of trains *de luxe*, and of personally con-
ducted tours, the dangers and the difficulties of a pilgrimage to
the Holy Land in the fifteenth century.   As Davies points out,
" It required, in the first place, a well-filled purse, then sufficient
leisure, a strong stomach, and, not least, a large amount of faith
in the efficacy of the undertaking.   Such indulgences as were
promised, and each different place had its own value, were well
earned, and probably were considered to well balance the incon-
veniences of extortion, *mal de mer*, vermin and bad food and
accommodation, which, with the great heat of the desert, caused
much ill-health, in many cases, death."   The illustrations in
the book were all drawn on the spot by Erhart Reuwich of
Utrecht, who accompanied the party.   They consist of some
large folding panoramic views of the places visited, pictures of
the costumes of the inhabitants in some cases, and cuts showing
various alphabets, such as Arabic, Hebrew, Greek, Syriac,
Coptic, Ethiopic, and Armenian.   Martin Martinez de Ampies
was the translator of this, the only Spanish edition of the work.
He has added a good deal to the original text by voluminous
notes, which make this edition substantially different to any
previous one.   To those who are acquainted with fifteenth-
century illustrated books, the first edition of the *Breidenbach*,
printed at Mainz in 1486, is one of the show books of the
century.   This Spanish issue has most, if not all, of the original
cuts which appeared in 1486, with many additional ones, some
copied from other books and some of original Spanish design.
Matthew Huss of Lyons has been laid under contribution, several
of the cuts from his *Voragine* of 1486 reappearing in this Spanish
Breidenbach.   Some others of Spanish provenance had already
illustrated the *Tesoro de la pasión* of Andres de Li, printed by

Si claſſem ꝟgo claudia ad litus tra
.bere valet cur ſpūſancto grauida vir
go nõ generaret.aug.de ciuitate dei
r.capı. lv. Zitus liuius de origine

Caladrius ſi facie egrum ſanare va
let. cur ꝛ̃pm ſaluatoꝛeȝ virgo nõ gene
raret. Jn de ꝓꝓꝛietatibꝰ reȝ libꝛo.ꝛij.
capı.

Si ferrum vi magnetis aer tenere va
let. cur pꝛedictum a pꝛophetis virgo
non generaret.Experiétia ꝓ calcidi
us de natura lapidum.

Pellicanus. ſi ſanguine animare feꝗ
tus apparet. cur ꝛ̃pm puro ſanguine
virgo non generaret yſidoꝛus.ri.

FIG. 25.—*Defensorium inviolatae virginitatis Mariae* [Zaragoza, Pablo Hurus, *c.* 1495].

Pablo Hurus in 1494. Among these cuts are some very good Spanish adaptations from what is known as the "Delbecq-Schreiber Passion," a series of twenty cuts which had appeared *c.* 1480. The "Scourging of Christ" (Fig. 26) and the

FIG. 26.—Andres De Li—*Tesoro de la pasión*, Zaragoza, Pablo Hurus, 1494.
Also,
Breidenbach—*Viaje de la tierra sancta*, Zaragoza, Pablo Hurus, 1498.
Also,
Nebrissensis—*Aurea Expositio Hymnorum*, Zaragoza, G. Coci, 1520.
Also,
Pedro de la Vega, *Flos Sanctorum*, Zaragoza, G. Coci, *c.* 1521.

"Driving out of the money changers" (Fig. 27) are typical examples. These cuts appear again in other books well on into the sixteenth century.

We may pause here to consider the wonderful example, afforded by this group of Zaragoza books, of the transference of

woodcuts among the early printers. Professor A. W. Pollard
has dealt with the general subject in a fascinating article which
appeared in *Bibliographica* (vol. ii., p. 343), but without any
special reference to Spain, which presents perhaps the most
remarkable instance of this habit of pictorial plagiarism. When
we consider that the actual blocks originally used in Ulm, Augs-

FIG. 27.—Andres De Li—*Tesoro de la pasión*, Zaragoza, Pablo Hurus, 1494.

burg, Nuremberg, Basel, and Lyons have found their way to
Zaragoza and other Spanish towns, we are put upon inquiry as to
the cause of so striking a phenomenon. The answer cannot be
merely that certain German printers emigrated to Spain and
brought the blocks with them. In some isolated cases this may
have been so, but the practice was too widespread and the places
of origin too far apart to allow of any such easy solution. I can

only suggest that a consideration of the medieval trade routes throughout Europe will furnish an explanation.   In the fifteenth century there was a recognised trade route from Germany through the southern parts of France to Spain, the chief stations on the way being Basel and Lyons.   What is more natural than that by purchase or barter the Spanish printer should provide himself with material at once adequate, and in all probability cheap.   And this must be said for him, that he exercised very excellent taste in his selection.   For example, it would be difficult, if not impossible, to improve upon the quality of the cuts which came from the wood-cutters of Ulm and Augsburg between 1470 and 1480.   The subject is one of great interest, but would necessitate much detailed and expert research to explore in an adequate way, as the available material is scattered far and wide among the libraries of Europe and America.

CHAPTER III.

BARCELONA.

PRINTING commenced in Barcelona in 1475. From 1481 to 1499 the most important printer in the town was Pedro Posa,

FIG. 28.—Gerson—*Imitacio Christi*, Barcelona, P. Posa, 1482.   (Reduced.)

a Catalan priest, and one of the most prolific native printers of the period.   The title-page of his *Imitacio Christi* in 1482 (Fig. 28), shows that he was capable of producing fine decorative work. The border used in it appears again in his *De partibus orationis*

(41)

by Phocas, and the very fine design of Italian knot work is an
almost exact reproduction of the border on the title of the
Calendarium of Regiomontanus, produced by Ratdolt at Venice
during the same year.   We find this border again at Barcelona,
eleven years later, in a *Vida e transit de San Jerónimo*, printed by
Pedro Miquel in 1493 (Haebler, 682), which has also a very
striking cut on the verso of the title, depicting Christ carrying
the Cross (Fig. 29).

The next Barcelona press to be mentioned is that of Juan
Rosembach.   A German from Heidelberg, he is one of the
most important and intriguing figures in the history of the
Spanish printing press.   Haebler attributes to him in the fifteenth
century eighteen books at Barcelona, five at Tarragona, two at
Valencia, and one at Perpignan.   I very much doubt if this at
all exhausts the number of his incunabula, while it is certain that
during the first thirty years of the sixteenth century he had a
very considerable output, Dr. Burger[1] giving some thirty-three
books printed by him between 1501 and 1530.

I think, however, it will be found, whenever an adequate
census of his books has been compiled, that these numbers will
be very considerably increased.   Sr. Don Pau Font y Rubinat, of
Reus, whose collection of books printed by Rosembach is unrivalled, has several examples hitherto unrecorded, and it is greatly
to be hoped that he will find time to place on record, in a permanent form, his very special knowledge of the work of this
printer.

In his *Peccador remut* of Malla, printed about 1495, which
book, however, does not contain his name, he uses a large ornamental title label, which is supported by the figures of two
angels.[2]   He uses it again in one of his acknowledged books, the

---

[1] Dr. Konrad Burger, *Die Drucker und Verleger in Spanien und Portugal von* 1501-
36, Leipzig, 1913, pp. 60-61.

[2] For reproduction, see Haebler, *The Early Printers of Spain and Portugal*
(Pl. III. (b)).

FIG. 29.—*Vida e transit de San Jerónimo*, Barcelona, Pedro Miquel, 1493.

Missale Tarraconense, printed at Tarragona in 1499 (Fig. 30). One of the best examples of Rosembach's illustrated fifteenth-century books is the *Carcel de amor* of San Pedro, which appeared in 1493 (Haebler, 606).

The cut on the title, representing a prison, in which love is supposed to be confined, has not much, if any, artistic merit, but has often been reproduced, no doubt as an example of the

FIG. 30.—*Missale Tarraconense*, Tarragona, Juan Rosembach, 1499.

fifteenth-century Spanish title-page, which so often evinces the maximum of decoration with the minimum of letterpress. In this instance, the xylographic title, consisting of three words in a scroll, being all, and one is bound to say, sufficient information, as to the contents of the book. The other sixteen cuts which appear in the text, are in an entirely different category. They are specially well executed and designed, and I do not hesitate to place them in the first rank of early Spanish woodcuts. Two of them are here reproduced from the copy in the British

Museum (G. 10225) which is the only one known to exist (Figs. 31 and 32).[1]

In 1495, he printed the *Libre de les dones* (Haebler, 706) of Franc. Ximenes, the very striking title-page of which is reproduced (Fig. 33).

FIG. 31.—San Pedro—*Carcel de amor*, Barcelona, Juan Rosembach, 1493.

As has already been mentioned, Rosembach's work extended well on into the sixteenth century. We find him principally engaged in Barcelona, with occasional excursions to Perpignan, Tarragona, and Montserrat. It was to the monastery at

[1] For other reproductions of these cuts, see the *Revista de Bibliografía Catalana*, vols. ii. and iv., 1902 and 1904.

Montserrat that he sent a staff of men to carry out liturgical printing there during the years 1518 to 1522, and again in 1524.   Of
his earlier work in the sixteenth century, his *Vocabulari molt profitos*

FIG. 32.—San Pedro—*Carcel de amor*, Barcelona, Juan Rosembach, 1493.

per apendre Lo Catalan Allamany y Lo Allamany Catalan, printed
at Perpignan, in 1502, has a good woodcut on the title, and the
colophon is followed by his small, and rather striking device

FIG. 33.—Franc. Ximenes—*Libre de les dones*, Barcelona, Juan Rosembach, 1495.

(Fig. 34).   The *Libre de cōsolat tractāt dels fets maritims*, etc.,
printed in the same year at Barcelona, is a fine piece of work.   It
has a remarkable cut of a ship on the title-page, where a sailor is
to be seen climbing the mast in apparent pursuit of the moon !
(Fig. 35), but this came from the press of J. Luschner.

Seculozum
Amen.

Stāpat lo pzesent
Vocabolari en la
noble vila de Per
pinya p mestre Jo
han Rosembach.
Any.ꝰꝰ.d.e dos.

On ende
Amen

Gedzulzt ist diser
vocabolari in der
edlē stat zu perpm
ia von meister han
sen Rosēbach Jm
Jar. ꝰꝰ.d.vñ.ii.

Fig. 34.—*Vocabulari*, Perpignan, Juan Rosembach, 1502.

Rosembach   printed   the   *Compendi   utilissim   cōtra   pestilēcia,*
printed in 1507, an exceedingly rare book, which has cuts of our
Lord and St. Sebastian on the title (Fig. 36).

The *Spill de la vida religiosa* which he produced in Barcelona
in 1515 and the *Gramatica Llatina* of Nebrissensis in 1523, are
two books in which his decorative title-pages are seen to advantage.

Libre de cõsolat tractat dels fets maritims zc.

FIG. 35.—*Libre de cõsolat*, Barcelona, J. Luschner, 1502.

Of his later work good specimens are the *Vita Christi del Seraphich doctor sanct Ioan Bonaventura* in 1522, the *De puerorum moribus disticha* of Michael Verinus, 1526, and his last recorded book, the *Ordinarium Tarraconense*, Barcelona, 1530.

The *Vita Christi*, in Catalan, has been a fruitful source of perplexity to bibliographers for many years. On the title-page, there is a cut of the Virgin and Child, with a figure in adoration, the word " Montserrat " being engraved at the foot, while in the bottom border two angels are busily plying a saw across a minia-ture mountain (Fig. 37). V. Salvá, in a catalogue of books issued by him in London in 1826, offered a copy for sale, to which he added the following note : " There is neither date, place, nor printer's name affixed to this edition, but from the type and the engraving on the title-page, I have no doubt that it was printed at the monastery of Montserrat about the year 1500. I do not find this work mentioned in Nicolás Antonio, nor, strange to say, in the diffuse account which Méndez gives in his *Tipografía es-pañola* of the editions printed at the monastery of Montserrat."

Hidalgo, who brought out another edition of Méndez in 1861, places this book among a list of doubtful ones. In 1904 Haebler, in his *Bibliografía Ibérica* (No. 70), attributes it to Rosembach at Barcelona, *c.* 1494. Between 1911 and 1915 re-productions of some of the cuts in the book are given in *Bibliofilia* (vol. i., p. 208, and vol. ii., pp. 114-15), and the book placed at Montserrat, *c.* 1518. As late as 1919, Albareda, in his *La im-premta de Montserrat*, describes the book at considerable length, and comes to the conclusion that all the available evidence sup-ports the Montserrat provenance, and urges in aid of his contention that the same cut on the title appears in a *Lectionarium*, admittedly printed by Rosembach at the monastery in 1524, and he places the *Vita Christi* at Montserrat between 1519 and 1522.

Haebler, speaking of Rosembach, has said, " his productions have only survived in some single specimens of great rarity." It is no doubt due to the rarity of books from this press that for so

Compendi vtilissim cõtra pestilécia tret dela font de

medicina. E conte ensi dotze auisos molt notables
per los quals mijansant lo diuinal adiutori quiscu
seguint aqlls: sia preuuada dela pestilécia. Amen.

FIG. 36.—*Compendi utilissim cõtra pestilécia*, Barcelona, Juan Rosembach, 1507.

many years, the date of this particular one and the place where it was printed, have been unknown.   Five copies have been recorded, four of them in Catalonia, and one in the British Museum. All of them were more or less imperfect, and uniformly so in the absence of the last leaf, containing the colophon and printer's device.   Some months ago, an elderly gentleman, staying in a London hotel, brought a copy of this book to a London bookseller, which he stated a friend, to whom it belonged, wished to sell, and further that it had been in the friend's family house in France for over fifty years.   As is usual with vendors of this class, anything in Gothic type with crude illustrations, and bound in old limp vellum, is considered to be of priceless value.   The bookseller was unimpressed with the book.   Its condition was indifferent, some leaves being missing, and its bibliographical importance, not unnaturally, being unknown to him.   Fortunately, he remembered that he had a customer, to whom anything " early Spanish " should be reported.   Eventually, the present owner was able to get into touch with the actual vendor, and one summer afternoon, in a second floor back office, in a side street, off a busy London thoroughfare, the book changed hands in an atmosphere which was certainly not literary, and at a price, high, but not too high, when the missing last leaf was found intact (Fig. 38), in its proper place, and thus the bibliographical doubts of a century were finally set at rest.

The book was in fact printed by Juan Rosembach at Barcelona, 8th February, 1522.   The printer's device used in this book is more elaborate than the usual white initials on the black background, which, with an intertwined " H," to denote Heidelberg, from which town he came, was the simple mark which Rosembach used in all his incunabula and in the large majority of his later books.   In this device, however, we have the Arms of Burgundy hanging from the branches of a tree, while two stags support a shield, round which is a motto and also his name.

The cuts in the book are crude, but not without interest.

Uíta Chríſti del Sera
phích doctoꝛ ſanct Joan Bonauentura
traduhít de latí en romanç:a gran vtíli-
tat dels deuots quí enla vída y paſſío de
noſtre redēptoꝛ contemplar deſígen:per
vn deuot relígíos del moneſtír de Mont
ſerrat dꝛla oꝛde de ſanct Benet.

FIG. 37.—S. Bonaventura—*Vita Christi*, Barcelona, Juan Rosembach, 1522.
(Original printed in red and black.)

¶ A lahor e gloria de nostre senyor
deu: e dla gloriosa verge maria mare sua: senyo
ra nostra. Es finida ab grā diligencia: la d
uota obra anomenada Vita christi de
sant Bonauentura. Estampat enla
insigne ciutat de Barçelona :
per mestre Joan Rosembach alemany. En
lany dela Incarnacio d no
stre seyor deu: a. viij
del mes de Fe
brer. Mil. D
y. rrij.

FIG. 38.—S. Bonaventura—*Vita Christi*, Barcelona, Juan Rosembach, 1522.
(Device of printer.)

The crucifixion on the verso of the title has character, while the little cut, depicting Christ stilling the tempest, does more credit

FIG. 39.—S. Bonaventura—*Vita Christi*, Barcelona, Juan Rosembach, 1522.

FIG. 40.—Verenus—*De puerorum moribus disticha*, Barcelona, Juan Rosembach, 1526.

to Barcelona shipbuilding in the sixteenth century than to any vessel in use in the time of our Lord (Fig. 39).

The *De puerorum moribus disticha* of 1526 is also a scarce little book, with its xylographic title, printed in red, followed

by a quaint little cut of the Evangelist Luke, whose connection
with the work is not very obvious (Fig. 40).

The last example of the printer is provided by the *Ordinarium Tarraconense*, a fine piece of liturgical printing ; the title,
which is printed in red, consists of a large " T " within a shield
(Figs. 41 and 42).

The illustrated books printed by Rosembach are characterised by a rugged simplicity, which is at once pleasing and
adequate.   Typically Spanish in atmosphere, his decorative
borders and illustrations were lavishly employed, and unlike most
of his contemporaries, the large majority of his fifteenth-century
books contain illustrations.

When we come to printing at Montserrat we shall have
something to say about Johann Luschner, but here in Barcelona
he also produced several books in the years 1495-1505.   His
illustrations are remarkably few, but I have a copy of the *Directorium inquisitorum* of Nicolaus Eymericus, printed by Luschner
28th September, 1503, in which, on the verso of the title, there is
a fine full-page cut of our Lord, with the legend, " Salvator mūdi
salva nos," and at the four corners the emblems of the Evangelists
(Fig. 43).   It is impressive and well designed, but what strikes
one most in the book is the number of very finely designed and
beautifully executed initial letters, white on a black background
(Fig. 44).   This is the first edition of one of the earliest works
on the practice of the Inquisition.   The author was a famous
Catalan theologian, who in addition to being chaplain to Pope
Gregory XI., was also appointed Chief Inquisitor in Aragon in
1356.   This work was reprinted in Rome in 1578, and there
were later editions.   Mr. Huth had a copy on vellum of this
first edition, which passed into the possession of Mr. C. Fairfax
Murray, and at his Sale it was bought by Quaritch, and is now
back again in Spain.   No other copy has been recorded until the
writer acquired one on paper in Barcelona in 1924.

Gabriel Pou printed an edition of the *Aeneid* of Virgil in

FIG. 41.—*Ordinarium Tarraconense*, Barcelona, Juan Rosembach, 1530.
(In original the title and shield are printed in red, the borders in black.)

¶Explicit ordinarium de mininiſtratione
ſacramētorum ſecūdum ritum et con-
ſuetudinem ſancte Metropolis
eccleſie Tarracoñ.maxima dili-
gentia ordinatum et cor-
rectum cuz nonnullis
operibᵘ vtiliſſimis in
ſertū.Impreſſuz
Barchinone
per magi-
ſtrum Johanez Roſembachale-
manum die.vij.mēſis febzuarij,
Anni.M.D.xxx.

FIG. 42.—*Ordinarium Tarraconense*, Barcelona, Juan Rosembach, 1530.
(Original printed in red and black.)

FIG. 43.—Eymericus—*Directorium inquisitorum*, Barcelona, Johann Luschner, 1503.

Barcelona, which survives in only a single copy in the British Museum.   It bears the date of 1405, which is of course absurd. Haebler strongly questions whether the book was printed in the fifteenth century at all, and suggests 1505 as more probable. Dr. Thomas, in his "Short-Title Catalogue of Books Printed in Spain and now in the British Museum," hazards the opinion that it may be 1495.   I incline to think that Haebler is correct.   There is no evidence at all, apart from the date on this Virgil, that Pou ever printed in the fifteenth century.   His other known books were in 1503, 1505, and 1507, and I have

FIG. 44.—Eymericus—*Directorium inquisitorum*, Barcelona, Johann Luschner, 1503.

recently secured another one in Barcelona, dated 1504.   It is an edition of the Constitutions of Catalonia, in Catalan, and the austere simplicity of the title-page (Fig. 45), and the neat form of his device (Fig. 46), which has now come to light for the first time, merit attention.   You will observe the representation of a well at the foot, and it is of interest to note that the Catalan word for our word " well " is " pou."   There is a small woodcut capital " P " in the text, which is identical with one in the Virgil, and I think we may now safely exclude Gabriel Pou from the number of fifteenth-century printers.   If this book of 1504 had been undated, even those acquainted with the archaic appearance of

Fig. 45.—*Constitucions*, Barcelona, Gabriel Pou, 1504.

Spanish printing well on into the sixteenth century might have dated the book ten years earlier.

We will conclude our survey of Barcelona printers by referring to a very rare edition of *La historia de las amors e vida del cavallre paris : e de viana filla del dalfi de franca*, which is attributed to the press of Diego Gumiel at this town *c.* 1494 (Haebler, 515(5)). We reproduce the very interesting device which appears on the title-page (Fig. 47). This device is one that was used by Pedro Posa and, if the attribution to Gumiel is correct, it must have passed into his possession. The book only survives in an imperfect copy which is now in the Library of the Institut d'Estudis Catalans at Barcelona.

Oeo gratias. Les presents cõstitu
cions foren empremta des en Barcelona
per gabriel Pou libre ter a .vij. de Febrer
del any mille sinch cen ts y quatre

FIG. 46.—*Constitucions*, Barcelona, Gabriel Pou, 1504.
(Device of printer.)

¶ Paris e viana.

FIG. 47.—*Paris E Viana* [Barcelona, Diego Gumiel, *c.* 1494].

Retablo dela vida de
cristo fecho en metro
por vn deuoto frayle
de la cartuxa.

FIG. 48.—Padilla—*Retablo de la vida de cristo*, Seville, Jacobo Cromberger, 1518.
Also (without the borders),
Cavalca—*Espejo de la Cruz*, Seville, Ungut & Polono, 1492.

CHAPTER IV.

SEVILLE, SALAMANCA AND BURGOS.

WE have already seen that the first illustrated book printed in Spain was produced at Seville. As far as the Seville printers of incunabula are concerned, book illustration was not their strong point. The work of Puerto and Segura has already been mentioned (p. 3). The Compañeros Alemanes,[1] an original quartet, who between 1490 and 1503 issued many books and shed individual partners from time to time, until Pegnitzer alone was left, contented themselves with single cuts to adorn their title-pages, the first of which did not appear until 1498, eight years after the commencement of the partnership.

The *Cronica del Cid* afforded them, or rather the three then remaining partners, the opportunity of displaying the martial valour of the Cid, Ruy Diaz de Bivar, on horseback on the first page, and one or two other similar examples can be found.

Meinardo Ungut and Stanislao Polono were similarly un-enterprising, but their *Cinco libros de Seneca* of 1491 has some fine decorative initials printed in red which are not common at the period. In 1492, in Cavalca's *Espejo de la cruz*, there is a cut on the verso of the title which is reproduced by Haebler,[2] and which I have found later in Padilla's *Retablo de la vida de cristo*, printed by Jacobo Cromberger in 1518, an unrecorded edition (Fig. 48).

[1] i.e. Paul of Cologne, Johann Pegnitzer, Magnus Herbst, and Thomas Glockner.
[2] Haebler, *The Early Printers of Spain and Portugal* (Pl. XXII.).

The *Processionarium ordinis praedicatorum* of 1494, one of
the earliest books with music printing in Spain, is a fine piece
of work.   The first woodcut capital letter, white on a red

FIG. 49.—*Processionarium*, Seville, Ungut and Polono, 1494.

background, with which the book opens, is a delicate and
interesting example of contemporary decoration (Fig. 49).   The
music notes are printed in black on a stave of four red lines, and

FIG. 50.—*Processionarium*, Seville, Ungut and Polono, 1494.

the book has at the end the pretty device of these printers, consisting of their initials, "M & S," hanging from the branches
of a tree (Fig. 50).   In 1500 Polono printed an edition of the
Improbatio Alcorani of Ricoldus, on the title of which a Friar

FIG. 51.—Ricoldus—*Improbatio Alcorani*, Seville, Stanislao Polono, 1500.

is depicted in the act of teaching five attentive, if somewhat plain-looking, Arabs (Fig. 51). His device appears in this book for the first time.

He seems to have emigrated to Alcalá in 1502, because we find that he printed the first book in that town in that year. A translation of the *Vita Christi* of Ludolphus de Saxonia by Ambrosio Montesino, it is a handsome work in four large and beautiful volumes. A bold Gothic type, printed

FIG. 52.—Ludolphus de Saxonia—*Vita Christi*, Alcalá, Stanislao Polono, 1502.

throughout in red and black, fine woodcut capitals, with his own interesting device, a cross and circle, the circle being doubled, with the initial "S" in the inner compartment and the word "Polonus" between the two circles, with a background of floral decoration (Fig. 52). On each of the four titles of the book there is a cut, which shows Montesino presenting his translation to the Catholic monarchs, Ferdinand and Isabella (Fig. 53). The whole work forms a fitting introduction to the art of printing in a town which in the years that followed was

FIG. 53.—Ludolphus de Saxonia—*Vita Christi*, Alcalá, Stanislao Polono, 1502.
(Reduced, original 245 × 171 mm.)

FIG. 54.—Boccaccio—*Fiameta*, Salamanca [Segundo grupo gótico], 1497.

FIG. 55.—Livy—*Las Decadas*, Salamanca [Segundo grupo gótico], 1497.

destined to take so important a place in both the typographical and the literary history of Spain.

Pedro Brun, who worked in conjunction with Juan Gentil at Seville, need not detain us at any length. Of his six books, only three have cuts, and of these, the best is probably the *Vespasiano* of 1499, which has some fine cuts, copied from the Lisbon edition of the same work, printed by Valentine Fernandez in Portuguese in 1496, and of which only one copy has survived. It has very justly been said that this book is worthy of reproduction in facsimile. It is easy to see from the reproduction of one of the cuts from the Spanish edition,[1] that the Portuguese originals must have been of very special merit.

The first press was established in the city of Salamanca in or about the year 1480, and was an anonymous one, nor did it, as far as is known, include any illustrated books. It is not until 1491 that we find another press, also anonymous, known as the "Segundo grupo gótico," containing books with any attempt at decoration or illustration. The outstanding production from this press, as far as woodcuts are concerned, is an edition of the *Evangelios y Epistolas*, printed in 1493, which exists in only one recorded copy in the University Library of Upsala. The cuts are crude and archaic, and are found in the first half of the book. There are fifty-seven in all, of which thirteen are repeated. Averaging 57 × 62 mm., they are mostly within very plain side borders and represent various scenes in the life of Christ. To judge from the reproductions given by Mr. Isak Collijn, in his excellent account of this book,[2] the cut of Christ's entry into Jerusalem, is perhaps the one in which crudeness is least apparent, and the text relating to this particular incident commences with a specially fine capital C, which is made up of delicate floral decoration in white, on a black background, a form of decoration which later on is found in several of the books from this press.

[1] Haebler, *The Early Printers of Spain and Portugal* (Plate XXVI.).
[2] Isak Collijn, *Notas sobre un incunable Español Desconocido*, Madrid, 1906.

FIG. 56.—Madrigal—*Confessional*, Salamanca [Segundo grupo gótico], 1498.

FIG. 57.—Deza—*Cōstituciões y Estatutos*, Salamanca [Segundo grupo gótico], 1501.

**Uita ꝛ processus sancti thome
cantuariensis martyris su-
per libertate ecclesiastica.**

FIG. 58.—*Vita et processus sancti thome cantuariensis*, Salamanca, Juan Giesser, 1506.
(Reduced, original 129 × 99 mm.)

FIG. 59.—Donatus—*De octo partibus orationis*, Burgos, Fadrique de Basilea, 1498.

Among the other cuts, a specially repulsive looking "devil" is used to illustrate the Temptation.   Space does not permit us to mention more than four other books from this press.   The *Fiameta* of Boccaccio in 1497, *Las Decadas* of Livy in the same year, the *Confessional* of Madrigal (El Tostado) in 1498, and a hitherto unrecorded edition of the *Cŏstituciões y Estatutos* of Diego de Deza, bishop of Palencia in 1501.

The *Fiameta* is a very rare book, of which the Salvá copy is now in the Pierpont Morgan Library in New York.   Its title-page, which represents Pánfilo and Fiameta, is a striking piece of work (Fig. 54).

The title-page of *Las Decadas* of Livy shows the author at work, and is one of the best cuts in any Salamanca book of the period (Fig. 55).

Madrigal's *El Confessional* of 1498 must not be confused with another edition issued in 1499 from the same press, although they both have the same full-page cut on the verso of the title (Fig. 56).

The *Cŏstituciões y Estatutos* of Deza is a discovery of my own, and the title-page is a typical piece of Spanish decoration with its xylographic title surmounted by the Bishop's Arms (Fig. 57).   It has also good initial letters of delicate workmanship, while the press work shows off to advantage the fine round Gothic type of these printers.

Juan Giesser, the last of the Salamanca printers of incunabula, had no illustrated books until the *Vita et processus sancti thome cantuariensis*, which he produced in 1506 (Fig. 58).

Burgos is the next town that claims our attention.   Printing was introduced there in 1485 by Fadrique (Biel) de Basilea, who had printed at Basel from 1470.   His device, we shall see later, is a lion holding in his paw a standard bearing the arms of that city.   He worked at Burgos for the long period of over thirty years (1485-1517), but it was some years after he commenced before he seriously directed his attention to the

FIG. 60.—Donatus—*De octo partibus orationis*, Burgos, Fadrique de Basilea, 1498.

FIG. 61.—Badius Ascensius—*Stultiferae naves* [Burgos, Fadrique de Basilea, *c.* 1501].

FIG. 62.—Badius Ascensius—*Stultiferae naves*, Paris, T. Kerver, 1500.

illustration of his books.   A book that he printed in 1498 deserves more than passing notice.   Among the school books of the fifteenth century, the Latin grammars of Aelius Donatus, a famous fourth-century grammarian, are to be found in numerous

Stultiferae naues sensus animof q3 trahentes mortis in exitium.

FIG. 63.—Badius Ascensius—*Stultiferae naves* [Burgos, Fadrique de Basilea, *c.* 1501].

editions in Germany, Italy, and the Low Countries, while in England editions have survived among our incunabula from the presses of Caxton, Machlinia, Wynkyn de Worde, and Pynson. So popular was this compressed grammar that we find editions among the block books long after the invention of printing by movable types, it being more economical to produce them

xylographically than to keep the type standing. Under these
circumstances, it is somewhat remarkable that there was only one

Stultarum uirginum scaphæ seu nauiculæ.
Contritura tuum persida supra caput.
Quæ quia supremo gnatum est paritura tonanti:
Commoda iustitiæ uincet origeneæ
Nam neq peccato quondam maculabitur ullo:
Nec deerit quæuis gratia uerbiparæ.
Currite fœstino fœlicia sæcula cursu:
Ut nouus in terris conspiciatur ada n.
Interea iugi pulchram certamine palmai :
Contra stultiferas quæso referte' uuhas.

Scapha stultæ uisionis ad stulti
feram nauem peruehens.

FIG. 64.—Badius Ascensius—*Stultiferae naves* [Burgos, Fadrique de Basilea, *c.* 1501].

edition in the fifteenth century printed in Spain, namely, the
De octo partibus orationis with the *Regula Dominus* of Remigius
added.

The author is exhibited at work in the cut which appears on the title (Fig. 59), and the first page of the text is within very striking and beautiful borders (Fig. 60), the decorative and sporting character of which, while having no obvious connexion with the study of grammar, no doubt afforded a pleasing distraction to the youthful students of the time.

The only other work of this printer which need detain us among his fifteenth-century books is his beautiful and extremely rare edition of the *Stultiferae naves* of Badius Ascensius, which appeared about 1499, and a copy of which is in the British Museum.   This work forms an addition to the famous *Stultifera navis* of Sebastian Brant, but the books are distinct, and should not be confused.   This Spanish edition has always been attributed to the year 1499, presumably because that year is engraved upon the device of Fadrique de Basilea, which is on the last leaf; but the book cannot have been printed until 1501, or possibly later. The first edition was printed in Paris, 22nd February, 1500 (i.e. 1500/01), and is, with some trifling exceptions in the setting, identical with this Burgos edition.   The cuts in the French edition are eight in number, and six of them are found closely reproduced in the Spanish edition.   I have examined the two books carefully, and there is no reasonable doubt that the Spanish cuts were in fact copied from the French and not vice versa. The Spanish wood-cutter has no doubt done his work well, but in his treatment he has not quite reproduced the minutiæ of the original.   Take, for example, the cut (Fig. 61) from the Spanish edition and note the waves, the shading, and the man at the extreme end of the boat on the left of the cut.   Now look at the same cut from the French edition (Fig. 62) and it will be seen that in the waves and shading the French is clearly more original, while you will notice that the man at the end of the boat at the left of the cut is engaged in putting a piece of food into his mouth, which was missed by the Spanish copyist, who has merely succeeded in giving him a double chin !

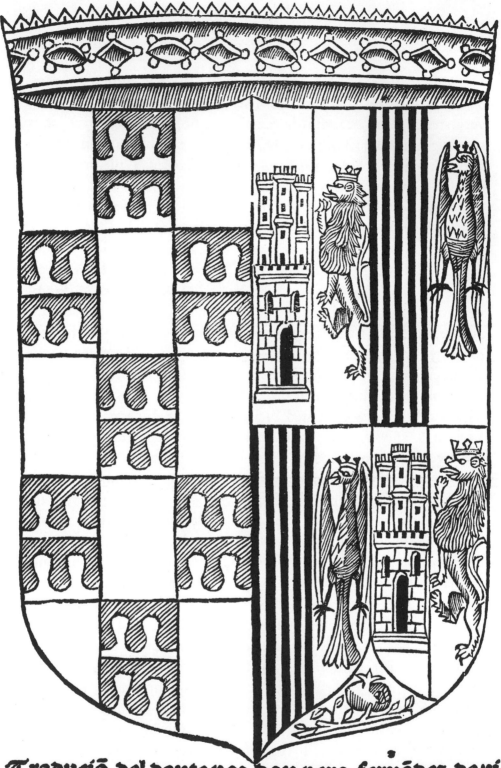

Traduciō del dante por don pero fernādez de vi
llegas dirigido ala señora dona Juana de aragō.

FIG. 65.—Dante—*El Infierno*, Burgos, Fadrique de Basilea, 1515.

Two other cuts from this Spanish edition are here reproduced, the one representing the mast of the boat as the tree of

ℂ Fue empꝛimido efte pꝛefente tratado en la muy noble y leal cibdad
de Burgos:poꝛ Fadꝛique aleman
de Bafilea Acauofe a.xxv.dias del
mes de Otubꝛe.Año de mill y quinientos y quinze años.⸭

FIG. 66.—*Refranes famosissimos*, Burgos, Fadrique de Basilea, 1515.
(Device of printer.)

the knowledge of good and evil, being an unusual treatment of
the subject (Fig. 63), while the one with the lady, with what
appears to be a looking-glass in her hand, and standing in the

boat, in which passengers are embarking, is an interesting piece of work (Fig. 64).

The French cuts reappeared in a translation entitled *La nef de folles* at Paris, "por petit Laurens Pour Geoffray de marnef," in 1500, while Michel le Noir uses them again in an edition in 1501.

Mention has been made of the date 1499 being engraved upon the device of the printer in this Spanish edition. How long this date was kept on this device I am not certain, but in the *Dante* which he printed in 1515 the date had by that time been removed from the scroll, the device being otherwise the same.

We will finish our consideration of the work of Fadrique de Basilea by referring to two of his later works, *El Infierno*, of Dante, and the *Refranes famosissimos*, both of which appeared in 1515.

El Infierno is the first edition of Dante printed in Spanish, and is a finely printed book, of importance and some rarity. A substantial folio volume, the title-page, mainly printed in red, with a large initial letter, into which two more or less grotesque heads are introduced, is very French in treatment. There is a large cut of the Arms of that unfortunate Queen, "Juana la loca," to whom the work is dedicated by the translator, Fernandez de Villegas (Fig. 65).

The device of the printer, to which reference has already been made, has on the verso of the leaf a cut of the Arms of the translator.

It may be seen again, in the reproduction of the colophon of his *Refranes famosissimos*, a work of extraordinary rarity, the only known copy of which was in the collection of the famous French bibliophile, Charles Nodier (Fig. 66). Here is the blank scroll where before had been inserted the date 1499. The device in this book is within a border. In the *Dante* it appears without one.

The next printer at Burgos was Juan de Burgos, who is

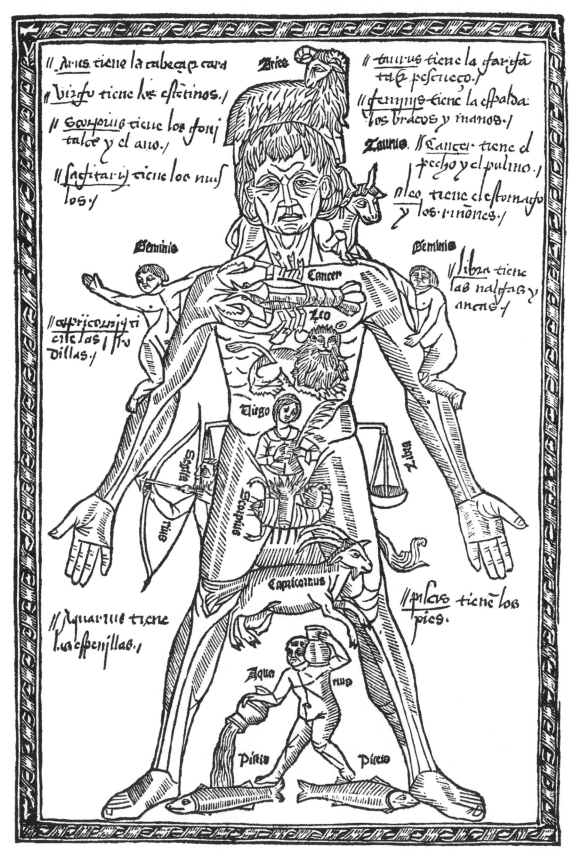

FIG. 67.—*Epiligo en medicina y cirurgia*, Burgos, Juan de Burgos, 1495.

responsible for several illustrated books between 1490 and 1499.
The three of which I have personal knowledge are the *Epiligo*

Aqui comiença vn tractado breue de confeſſion copila/
do por el maniſico arçobiſpo de palermo maeſtro en ſã
cta theologia E enel tiepo q̃ le copilo daba cruzada a to
dos los q̃ a el ocuriã con q̃ erã aſueltos de ſus peccõs •

l preſente tra
ctado es para
prouecho de
las animas t
para maniſeſtar las enfer
medades que ſon los pec/
cados por que no ſecoſton
pan t ſe podreſcan como
diſe dauit • q̃m tacui • t in
ueterauerũt oſſa mea • que
quiere deſir • por que calle
conuiene a ſaber mis peca
dos que no los confeſſe ſe
enueiecieron mis hueſſos
q̃ ſon mis virtudes • E en
otra pte diſe • putruerunt t
corrupte ſunt cicatrices mee a facie inſipiencie mee • que quiere deſir
podrecieronſe t fuerõ coſtonpidas mis llagas que ſon los peccados
õla faz de mi inorancia que es la verguêça por que no los confieſo •
E anſe eſtas enfermedades de maniſeſtar al medico q̃ es al ſacerdo/
te para q̃ las ſane t dela medecina ſegun fuere la calidad dela enfer
medad q̃ es q̃ nos de la penitencia ſegũ fuere el peccado • E por eſto
diſe boecio enel primero libro de cõſolacion • Si opera medicantis
eꝛpectas • Oportet vt vulnus detegas tuum • que quiere deſir ſi eſpe
ras medecina del medico conuienc q̃ deſcubras tu enfermedad • Aſſi
que qual quier fiel chriſtiano que quiſiere ſaber maniſeſtar o confeſ/
ſar ſus peccados lea eſte tractado • El qual empieça ha honor t ala
bança de dios t dela virgen ſu madre •   •a•

F IG. 68.—*Tractado breve de confession* [Burgos, Juan de Burgos, *c.* 1495].

en medicina y cirurgia of Ketham in 1495, *Un tractado breve de confession* of about the same period, and the *Doctrinal de caballeros* of Cartagena, printed by him in May 1497.

FIG. 69.—Cartagena—*Doctrinal de los caballeros*, Burgos, Juan de Burgos, 1497.
Also,
Livy—*Las Decadas*, Burgos, Andres de Burgos, 1505.
(With borders.)

The *Epiligo en medicina* is the first Spanish edition of this famous fifteenth-century collection of medical and surgical treatises written for the benefit of the general practitioners of

the time.   The book has many fine cuts, including a contemporary surgery with two doctors discussing the contents of a
flask of urine, while a specially clear full-page cut shows the
astronomical man (Fig. 67).   There are many other cuts in
the book, which combine to make it a striking picture of the
practice of medicine and surgery in the fifteenth century.

The *Tractado breve de confession* has no place, printer, or
date of printing.   I discovered it, bound up with another
Spanish incunable, both of them having been at one time in the
library of a religious house at Oristano in Sardinia.   On the title
there is a cut which represents the Pope, Alexander VI. (Rodrigo Borja), himself a member of a Spanish family settled near
Valencia, seated on his throne, presenting crosses to a number
of persons, one of whom is kneeling in the act of receiving it
(Fig. 68).   Dr. Haebler, when I submitted the book to him,
readily identified the types as those of Juan de Burgos, and dated
the book between 1495 and 1499.   He further tells me that
the cut has hitherto been unknown, and that he cannot trace it
in any other book, an unusual occurrence, as we have seen, in
the case of early Spanish woodcuts.

The *Doctrinal de caballeros* of Cartagena has a cut on the
title which represents a king seated on his throne in the act of
delivering a lance to a knight, who kneels before him (Fig. 69).
I have found this cut again in an edition of *Las Decadas* of Livy,
printed by Andres de Burgos, also at Burgos in 1505.

CHAPTER V.

TOLEDO, PAMPLONA, VALLADOLID AND MONTSERRAT.

TOLEDO has already been referred to as the place where Juan Vasquez started a press in 1484, by printing indulgences. He

FIG. 70.—*Bula de difuntos* (en Catalán) [Toledo, Antonio Tellez, 1495].

was followed by Antonio Tellez, who printed similar ecclesiastical documents and books. For example, I have a *Bula de difuntos* in Catalan, printed in 1495, in which there is a small circular cut, representing the Virgin and Child, and, alongside, woodcut reproductions of the signatures of the Bishops of Ávila

(89)

and Salamanca (Fig. 70).   The only other known copy of this indulgence, in a very mutilated state, is in the Biblioteca de Catalunya at Barcelona.

In 1498 Pedro Hagembach started a press in the town, which included several works, both sacred and profane, which were illustrated.

The *Comentarios* of Julius Cæsar, which appeared in 1498, has a good title-page with a well-designed cut of the Royal Arms.   An important historical and liturgical book, the *Missale Mixtum*, or Mozarabic Missal, is perhaps his "magnum opus." One of the most sumptuously printed of early Spanish books, there is a cut on the title representing St. Ildefonso receiving the *casula* at the hands of the Virgin, surmounted by a cross and crowned with a cardinal's hat.   This particular cut has been regarded by some bibliographers as depicting the arms of Cardinal Ximenes de Cisneros, and being used by Hagembach as his device.   It certainly does not represent the arms of the cardinal, which are correctly given in the Complutensian Polyglot Bible (Fig. 207).

Hagembach seems to have used the cut in two states.   In the *Comentarios* of Cæsar it appears without the border, motto, cross, or cardinal's hat, all of which are found in this missal. As the cut also appears in books which were not printed by him, the reasonable assumption is that it was used in books brought out under the patronage and direction of Ximenes, and it appears to have been confined to such books.   A fine crucifixion cut is reproduced from this Missal (Fig. 71).

Hagembach printed during the opening years of the next century, and *Las Epistolas de Seneca* in 1502, and *Los V libros* of the same author in 1510, both have a rather well-known cut of a man seated in a monastic scriptorium, or cell, at a table, engaged in writing, while on the wall in front of him is a shelf with an open book.   His *Scala spiritualis* of Climacus, which he printed in 1505, has the Ildefonso cut on the title, which we

FIG. 71.—*Missale Mixtum*, Toledo, Pedro Hagembach, 1500.

have already mentioned (Fig. 72). Up to the present it has always been assumed that Hagembach stopped printing in Toledo in 1505, but I am reasonably certain that even if his death had taken place by this time, that at least two later books were printed with his types, the *Los V libros* of Seneca in 1510, and the *Cayda de principes* of Boccaccio in 1511. The last-named book is a

Scala spiritualis sacti
Joannis Climaci.

FIG. 72.—Climacus—*Scala spiritualis*, Toledo [Pedro Hagembach], 1505.
(Reduced, original 157 × 92 mm.)

very interesting one, which has upon its title-page a most amus-ing cut showing the wheel of fortune. Four figures are portrayed in grotesque and humorous attitudes on various spokes of the wheel, which is being turned by a solemn-looking lady repre-senting "La Fortuna." For the period, a striking piece of artistic humour (Fig. 73). This cut appeared in an edition of the same work which was printed by Meinardo Ungut and Stanislao Polono in 1495. The original source from which this design

was copied is of special interest.   Among the beautiful designs
which adorn the wonderful pavement in Siena Cathedral is one

FIG. 73.—Boccaccio—*Cayda de principes*, Toledo, 1511.
(Reduced, original 220 × 151 mm.)

dating back to 1372 and depicting a wheel with eight spokes,
with a king at the top and three figures clinging to the two sides
and bottom, striving to maintain their hold as the wheel revolves.

In the outside angles of the design are portraits of Epictetus, Aristotle, Seneca, and Euripides, each with a scroll containing a quotation from his own writings.   In imitation of this, Domenico di Niccolo del Coro, who held the post of Clerk of the Works in the cathedral between 1413 and 1423, and was himself famous for his skill in carving and inlay, designed a Wheel of Fortune,

FIG. 74.—S. Bonaventura—*Diaeta salutis*, Pamplona, A. G. de Brocar, 1497.

which he inlaid in the lower panel of a door in the Chapel of the Palazzo Communale.   This design is practically the same as the Spanish woodcut.   At the bottom of the wheel a man is clinging, with the inscription *So senza Regno* (I am without a kingdom).   Half-way up the wheel on the right clings another figure, and the inscription, *Regnero* (I will reign).   On the top a seated figure with the word *Regno* (I reign), and lastly, on the other side, a man descending with the word *Regnai* (I have reigned). Reference to the cut will show that these inscriptions have all been copied and rendered into Spanish.[1]

The town of Pamplona had only one press in the fifteenth century, but the printer, Arnaldo Guillén de Brocar, who printed some sixteen books there before the close of the century, will ever be famous for his great Polyglot Bible and many other books which he printed in Alcalá and elsewhere in the sixteenth century, and to which attention will be directed later on.

Of his incunabula the *Diaeta salutis* of Bonaventura in 1497 is an interesting little octavo volume, which has a cut of the crucifixion on the title, and one of the Virgin and Child on the verso. The colophon, with an early example of his device is here reproduced (Fig. 74). That he was capable of producing a well-executed title-page can be seen from his *Doctrina de los religiosos en romançe* of Peraldus, which he printed in 1499. The features of the Friar, who is shown in a pulpit addressing some colleagues, show an unusual amount of expression, as do the faces of the congregation (Fig. 75).

Mention has already been made of Valladolid and of the press at the monastery of Nuestra Señora del Prado. Pedro Giraldi and Miguel de Planes were responsible in this city for many illustrated books during the last three years of the century. Their *Memoria de la redencion* of Pérez Machuca in 1497, for example, has a cut of the Royal Arms on the title, noticeable for the decorative floral work, of unusual distinction, which surrounds it (Fig. 76). Of this book there are only two known copies.

Montserrat is the last place we shall deal with in this outline of Spanish book-illustration in the fifteenth century. The monastery of Montserrat (mons serratus) is one of the most interesting places in the neighbourhood of Barcelona. The

[1] For an account of this Pavement of Siena, see R. H. Hobert Cust's *The Pavement Masters of Siena*, London, G. Bell & Sons, 1901.

mountain upon which the monastery is situated is indeed jagged
as a saw.   This peculiarity is a prominent feature of almost every

Fig. 75.—Peraldus—*Doctrina de los religiosos en romançe*, Pamplona, A. G. de Brocar,
1499.

cut that issued from the monastic press in the fifteenth century. The press started in 1499, and Juan Luschner, whose work at

FIG. 76.—Pérez Machuca—*Memoria de la redencion*, Valladolid, Pedro Giraldi y Miguel de Planes, 1497.

Barcelona we have already noticed, was the first printer. His first book was the *Meditationes* of St. Bonaventura, one of a series

of that author's works.   They were small octavo volumes, of
which 800 copies of each seem to have been printed.

We will select as an example, the *De instructione Novitiorum*,
which was issued on the 16th June, 1499.

Albareda, in his bibliography (itself printed in the monas-

Fig. 77.—S. Bonaventura—*Instructione Novitiorum*, Montserrat, J. Luschner, 1499.

tery),[1] apologises for a brief description of the book, as in spite
of the original issue of 800 copies, he had found it difficult to find
a complete one.   The title-page shows the monastery and the
mountain (Fig. 77), while the circular cut which follows the
colophon depicts the Virgin and Child, who is engaged using a
saw upon one of the peaks of the mountain.   Luschner seems to

[1] Albareda, *La impremta de Montserrat*, 1919, pp. 90-92.

have produced some seventeen books at the monastery between 1499 and 1500. In all probability this does not exhaust his output. Haebler [1] gives an interesting account of a contract dated in January, 1499, between Luschner and the authorities of the monastery, in which the wages of himself and his men are provided for, and the prices of the printing material and paper fixed.

Juan Rosembach was another Barcelona printer who worked for the Montserrat press, as we find that between 1518 and 1524 he, by himself, or by his workmen, printed many liturgical works within the monastic walls. In the absence of surviving copies of many of these it will always be difficult to say with any degree of certainty whether in fact they were actually all printed there or at Rosembach's established press at Barcelona.

[1] *The Early Printers of Spain and Portugal*, pp. 76-77.

Indulgēcia ⁊ cofadria del hospital de señoz Santiago.

Pristi nomine ⁊ beati Jacobi inuocato. A todos sea manifiesto como el papa alexandzo lexto poz su bulla aplica dio facultad al Rey ⁊ ala reyna nuestros señozes pa instruyr. E sus altezas poz la dicha autoridad aplica instituyeró vna cofadzia pa siempze jamas enel hospital q̃ poz su mandado como patrones dl se haze enla cibdad d stiago. E otozga su stidad a todos los que dieren en limosna pa el edeficio dl dho hospital: ⁊ pa mātenimiēto dlos peregrinos. pobzes ⁊ éfcrinos q̃ eñl recibieren. la sexta parte d vn ducado: q̃ só sesēta ⁊ dos mf̄s ⁊ medio: q̃ sean cofadres ⁊ ganē las indulgēcias siguientes. C Pzimeramēte otozga pa siēpze a alquier cofad̄e o seruidoz ⁊ official dl hospital: q̃ pueda elegir confessoz cligo o religioso q̃ los absuelua d todos sus peccados. crimines ⁊ excessos. es asaber dlos reseruados vna vez enla vida except o ofésa dla libertad eclesiastica. eregia rebelió o cóspiracion contra la psona o estado dl papa ⁊ dla se aplica. falsedad letras apolicas. robo: ocupacion: destruyció dlas tierras ⁊ mar dla yglia d roma o dlas subjetas a ella. ofésa psonal cōtra obispo o otro plado. phibició dlas causas q̃ no se obuelua a cozte de roma: lleuar armas ⁊ otras cosas vedadas a tierras de infieles: ⁊ d todos los otros los absiuclua q̄ntas vezes dsierē: imponiēdo les penitēcia saludable. C Jtē q̃ los pueda absoluer a culpa ⁊ a pena vna vez enla vida ⁊ otta vez eñl articulo dla muerte d todos sus peccados plenariamēte de q̃ se ouieren cófessado: satisfaziēdo poz si o poz otro lo q̃ fuerē obligados. C Pero si alguno desistiere dela fe ⁊ obediēcia dla see apostolica: o poz cófiança d esta idulgencia pecasse. la cōcessió q̄nto a elegir cófessoz no le apzouecha. C Otrosi q̃ les pueda comutar q̄lesquier votos en otras obzas pias. excepto voto d jhr̄m: roma: stiago en cópostela. castidad. religió. C Otrosi les cócede q̃ visitādo có duoció do quier q̃ estouierē vna yglia enla q̄resma: o en otro alquier dia en q̃ se andan las estaciōs d roma: dizjēdo d rodillas duota mēte cico vezes el pater noster cõel aue maria: alancé todos ⁊ q̄lesq̃z idulgēcias ⁊pdofias ⁊ plenarias remissiofisq̃ ganā todos los q̃ psonalmēte vā a visitar las yglias ⁊ estaciofis dētro ⁊ dfuerad roma. como si en psona las dtuniesse ⁊ fuesse a ganar. C Otrosi les otozga cótritos ⁊ cófessados. q̃ visitādo alquier yglia d nfa señora ⁊ d señoz stiago en todas sus fiestas: o otra alquier yglia dōde estouierē dsde las primeras fasta las segūdas visperas: ganē poz cada fiesta treynta años ⁊ treinta q̄retenas d pdó. C Otrosi q̃ pueda dode: q̃ estouierē avn q̃ sea en tpo de entredcho ozdinario en q̄lesq̃z yglias q̃ dsieren cóla solenidad q̃ el derecho dispone: oyr missas ⁊ los diuinos oficios. ⁊ recebir los sacramētos ⁊ el corpus xp̄i. saluo enla pascua d resurecion: ⁊ si alguno fallesciere en tiempo de entredicho. le sea dada sin pompa sepultura eclesiastica: no seyendo causa del entredicho C Jten otorga alas mugeres q̃ puedē q̄tro vezes enel año có vna o dos onestas cópañeras entrar en alquier monesterio d mōjas o alqd̄e: ozden avn q̃ sea d sca clara encerradas: ⁊ comer cõellas: d cósentimiento d sus superiores: có q̃ no duerma noche ōtrō C Jtē otozga alos cofrades q̃ si mas pagaz q̃ sea pticipātes d todas las missas. sacrificios: oraciofis: ayunos. limofnas ⁊ pias obras q̃se fizieren pa siempze eñl dho hospital. E d mas dlas idulgencias dhas: otozga otras muchas q̃ los q̃ se fallarē eñl dho hospital. E poz q̃ vos   distes la suma suso dha al nūcio embiado có podez del administradoz dl hospital: gozays d todas las gracias ⁊ idulgencias suso dichas: cōtāto q̃ recibays la psente. ⁊ la tengays en vfo podez q̃ va cõel sello ⁊ firma dl administradoz. Dada a   dias dl mes de   Año de mill ⁊ quinientos ⁊ quatro años:

Forma plenarie absolutionis

Misereat tui omp̄s de⁹ ⁊c̄. Ego poz la autoridad d nfo señoz Jesu xp̄o ⁊ d sāt pedzo ⁊ de sant pablo ⁊ dl romano pōtifice a mi cometida: ⁊ poz la gfa ati fecha te absueluo plenamente a culpa ⁊ a pena d todos tus peccados cótritos ⁊ cófessados: a vn q̃ sea refuados ala see apostolica: ⁊ q̃ gozes dlas indulgencias ⁊ remissiofis dlas scās estaciofis d roma. q̃ poz vtud dsta sca indulgencia as cóseguido: lo q̄l todo sea pa en remissió d todos tus peccados. ⁊ pa cósecució dla vida pdurable. Jn noie patris ⁊ c̄: E enel articulo dla muerte diga el cófessoz. Si esta vez no fallescieres refuada te sea esta indulgencia para enel verdadero articulo dela muerte: Jn noie patris ⁊ filij ⁊ spiritussancti: Amen.

Fig 223*.—Alexander VI.—*Indulgēcia y cofadria del hospital de señor Santiago* [Logroño, A. G. de Brocar], 1504. (Reduced, original measures 278 × 177 mm.)

PART II.

THE SIXTEENTH CENTURY.

CHAPTER VI.

INTRODUCTION.

WE have discussed the illustrated books produced in some of the important towns during the fifteenth century. Printing was continued in these during the succeeding one, and in addition, in over thirty other towns, which had not before been the scene of any typographical activity. Among the more important of these are Alcalá, Logroño, Medina del Campo, Madrid and Segovia, while a town like Granada, where only one or two books were printed in the fifteenth century, had later on a considerable output.

It has been roughly estimated [1] that the actual number of books printed during the sixteenth century in Spain, not including books printed in the Spanish language elsewhere, was approximately 10,000. It will be readily seen therefore, that the material available for consideration is overwhelmingly greater than it was during the preceding century. It would be difficult, if not impossible, within the limits of space at our disposal, to do more than deal with the more important towns and printers, and attempt, however inadequately, to outline the progress of book illustration and the decoration of the printed page, during this momentous century. Momentous it was, in every sense of the

[1] Dr. H. Thomas, *The Output of Books in Spain in the Sixteenth Century* (*Bib. Soc. Transactions*, vol. xv., p. 155).

word, and for Spain, it included the golden age of her history in both the arts of peace and war.

It is not necessary to dwell upon the series of events, a long recital of warfare and intrigue, which resulted, after the marriage of Ferdinand of Aragon and Isabella of Castile, in an united and prosperous Spain, at the end of the fifteenth century. It is sufficient to say that by the end of the first quarter of the sixteenth century, Spain, under the Emperor, Charles V., was practically the unchallenged mistress of a large portion of Europe. The effects of the Italian renaissance had reached the Peninsula, mainly owing to the close and intimate relations existing between the two countries. Naples, owing to the military genius of " El gran capitan " (Gonzalvo de Córdova), was under Spanish rule. Temporarily, at any rate, Rome itself was under subjection to Charles V., and the Pope his captive. A large number of Spaniards were continually travelling through Italy, and many of them became permanent residents in all her large towns. Under these circumstances, it is little wonder that Spain should show manifest signs of the literary genius and taste of the Italy of the period. Juan de Boscan and Garcilasso de la Vega formed a new school of Spanish poetry, based upon Italian models. The Inquisition, might, and did repress and discourage scientific investigation, and every attempt to translate the Scriptures into the vernacular, but the historian was allowed a comparatively free hand, while the unknown author of *Lazarillo de Tormes*, produced the first picaresque novel, with results that were destined to react for long on the literature, not only of Spain, but of most of the other countries of Europe. Romances of chivalry, in the *Amadis* and *Palmerin* series, swept over the country in a veritable flood, and by the end of the century, and the beginning of the next one, had prepared the way for their antidote, in the shape of *Don Quixote*, the world's greatest novel, the work of Miguel de Cervantes Saavedra, Spain's immortal and unrivalled literary genius.

In the drama, Lope de Rueda and Juan de Cueva were the forerunners of Lope de Vega, the most prolific playwright of any country, or of any age.

Under the inspiration of Titian, we see Sanchez Coello, Pantoja and others, as pioneers in the field of her pictorial art, which later on was to witness the imperishable productions of a Velasquez and a Murillo. In colonisation, Spain was at her zenith. The New World placed rich tribute at her feet, and her ships, at any rate until 1588, held undisputed command of the seas.

In military matters, as has been indicated, she dominated Europe, but this century, which thus witnessed what was in very truth her golden age, before it had run its course, saw the commencement of an equally remarkable decline and fall. We shall see the same stages reflected in the work of the printing press in the pages that follow.

FIG. 78.—*La vida de Santa Magdalena*, Valencia, Juan Joffre, 1505.

CHAPTER VII.

VALENCIA.

VALENCIA was the birthplace of printing in Spain, and we have already noticed the work of her fifteenth-century printers. In the sixteenth century, the press of Juan Joffre was one of the most important in the city. He commenced to print in 1502, and continued for over a quarter of a century. We will select as examples of his work, *La vida de Santa Magdalena en cobbles* of Jaime Gazull (1505), *La vida de Sancta Catherina de Sena* (1511), the *Blanquerna* of Ramon Lull (1521) and the *Meditationes* of St. Augustine (1525).

The *Vida de Santa Magdalena*, an early example from this press in 1505, is profusely illustrated, and is one of the most artistic and remarkable illustrated books of the period. The first notice of any copy of it appeared in the catalogue of the collection of the Rev. Thomas Crofts, M.A., Chancellor of the Diocese of Peterborough, dispersed by public auction in London in 1783, a Sale which lasted for forty-three days.

In this catalogue, the authorship of the book was attributed to Gabriel Pellicer, and similarly by Brunet (vol. iv., p. 473). This Crofts copy passed into the collection of Salvá, and later into the possession of Heredia, at whose Sale in 1891, it was acquired for the Biblioteca Nacional at Madrid, for 500 francs, and is apparently the only known copy of the book. It is an octavo volume of sixty-two leaves in Gothic type. It contains no less than sixty full-page woodcuts, each within well-designed and different borders. The striking character of these cuts, so far in advance of the time at which they appeared, will be seen from the reproductions, which we are privileged to give by the courtesy of Sr. Don Miquel y Planas of Barcelona (Figs. 78, 79, 80, and 81).

La vida de Sancta Catherina de Sena, which Joffre printed

FIG. 79.—*La vida de Santa Magdalena*, Valencia, Juan Joffre, 1505.

in 1511, has some pleasing cuts, of which a specimen is reproduced (Fig. 82).

The *Blanquerna* of Ramon Lull, a book of quite considerable literary interest, and also a good example of the decorative

FIG. 80.—*La vida de Santa Magdalena*, Valencia, Juan Joffre, 1505.

work of Joffre, appeared in 1521.　The title, printed in red and
black, is within a decorative border, as are several other pages in

FIG. 81.—*La vida de Santa Magdalena*, Valencia, Juan Joffre, 1505.

the book, all of them being of interest and merit.　Three full-
page cuts also call for notice.

The first, on the verso of the title, represents Lull standing in a field, talking to a heavenly visitor, whose wings seem

FIG. 82.—*La vida de Sancta Catherina de Sena*, Valencia, Juan Joffre, 1511.

somewhat out of keeping with his sixteenth-century costume.
The second (fol. 8b) shows him addressing a young man and
woman, who are seated before him, on the subject of matrimony.
The third cut, which is to be found on the verso of the title

FIG. 83.—*Los Triumphos de Apiano*, Valencia, Juan Joffre, 1522.
(Reduced, original 235 × 178 mm.)

of the *Libre D'oracions* (which forms an appendix to the book),
portrays Lull kneeling in the act of receiving inspiration.
Allegorical in treatment, it is designed to illustrate the connexion between Understanding, Memory and Will, and the
corresponding physical organs of the Ear, Brain and Heart.   For

some unaccountable reason, this book, remarkable for its literary contents and for its typographical beauty, has escaped notice at the hands of either J. E. Serrano y Morales or J. Ribelles Comín, the two authorities on the Valencian printing press.

From *Los Triumphos de Apiano*, which appeared in 1522, we reproduce from the last leaf the mermaid device of Joffre, which he used in most of his books (Fig. 83). On the title,

FIG. 84.—S. Augustine—*Meditationes*, Valencia, Juan Joffre, 1525.

which is often found coloured by hand, there is a large cut representing the Arms of D. Rodrigo de Mendoza, to whom the work is dedicated by the translator, Juan de Molina.

The *Meditationes* of St. Augustine, produced in 1525, has a cut, obviously of earlier date than the book, showing the Saint standing with Mary and the Infant Christ (Fig. 84).

Iorge Costilla, who printed in the town from 1509 to 1531, was responsible in 1510 for the first Spanish edition of the chronicle of Johannes Philippus Foresti, of Bergamo. An

Augustinian monk, he was born in 1434 and died *c.* 1518. The book may be described as a supplementary volume designed to bring up to date the various encyclopedic works which had preceded it. For this reason, Bergomensis called it the *Supplementum Chronicarum*. Like the *Fasciculus temporum*, already referred to, it contains biblical cuts and views of cities. The first illustrated edition appeared in Venice in 1486 (Hain *2807), and numerous other editions were published later on in Italy, and showed progressive improvement in the design and execution of the illustrations.[1] This Spanish edition was translated by

FIG. 85.—Bergomensis—*Suma de todas las Cronicas del mundo*, Valencia, Iorge Costilla, 1510.

Narcis Viñoles, a Valencian poet, under the title, *Suma de todas las Cronicas del mundo*. The translator apologises in his preface for writing the work in Castilian, because " yo no hijo natural," and goes on to describe the various dialects of Spain as barbarous and savage in comparison with Castilian. The title-page is a striking piece of xylographic printing. One of the capital letters has a grotesque head, very similar to those found in the books of Antoine Verard, of Paris. The initial letters throughout the book are well executed, and of more than average decorative merit (Fig. 85). The cuts represent the usual subjects found in the previous Italian editions, but the Spanish influence can be seen in

[1] *Vide* Lippmann, *Wood Engraving in Italy in the Fifteenth Century*, 1888 (pp. 70-76).

most of them.   The one of the author, seated at a table, engaged in
writing the book, is markedly Spanish in treatment (Fig. 86).
Another, which depicts the expulsion from Paradise (Fig. 87),
although a conventional rendering of the subject, has a lizard
among the livestock in the garden, which takes the place of the
rabbit of the Italian artists, presumably because in sunny Spain

FIG. 86.—Bergomensis—*Suma de todas las Cronicas del mundo*, Valencia, Iorge
Costilla, 1510.

lizards were far more common.   The views of the cities are more
striking than accurate.   For example, we find three-fourths of
the view of Rome doing duty later on for Milan, and still later
for Antioch and Pisa !   Although the chronicle of events deals
with incidents as late as 1502, there is no reference to the discovery of America, which had been mentioned in the Venice
editions of 1503 and 1506.   The art of printing, however, is
attributed to either Gutenburg ("conteburgo") or Fust, in 1458.

Juan Navarro printed, in 1539, the first edition of the poems of Ausias March, the famous Catalan poet. A disciple of Petrarch, in the form he gave to his verse, he nevertheless had a marked style of his own, and evinced a feeling and moral sense which have secured for him a lasting and honoured reputation. The title-page of this first edition is enclosed within a border, which is a striking and pleasing example of contemporary work.

FIG. 87.—Bergomensis—*Suma de todas las Cronicas del mundo*, Valencia, Iorge Costilla, 1510.

The *Libro tercero de la chronyca de Valencia* of Martin de Vicyana appeared in 1564, and is a specimen of Navarro's later work, or possibly of that of his son. A book of some rarity, of which there is only an imperfect copy in the British Museum, it contains some interesting cuts. Among these, there is a Madonna and Child (fol. xxii), which has every appearance of having been taken from a block of a much earlier date. There is also a very remarkable one (fol. clxvi b) of the town and castle of Alicante. The rock is shown upon which the castle is situated, with a

FIG. 88.—M. de Vicyana—*Libro tercero de la chronyca de Valencia*, Valencia, Juan Navarro, 1564.

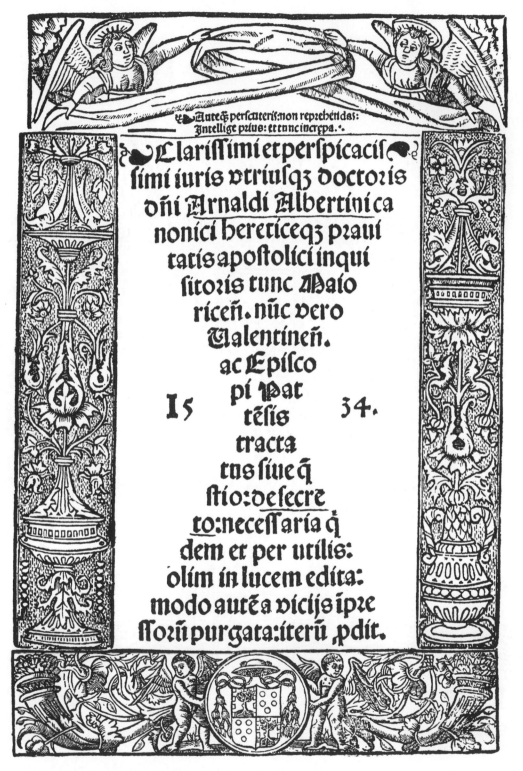

FIG. 89.—Albertinus—*Quaestio de secreto*, Valencia, Francisco Diaz, 1534.

strange formation in the shape of a man's head, which is described
in the text as "muy al proprio y natural" (Fig. 88). This rock
was blown asunder by the French in 1707, and to-day there is no
trace of this particular freak of nature.

Another Valencian printer, whose work merits attention,
was Francisco Diaz (Franciscus Romanus). His *Quaestio de
secreto*, of Arnaldus Albertinus, in 1534, is noticeable for a hand-

FIG. 90.—*Consulado del Mar*, Valencia, Francisco Diaz Romano, 1539.

some title-page (Fig. 89), and his Spanish edition of the *Consulado
del mar*, which he produced in 1539, has a cut on the title, showing some sailors worshipping the Virgin, and another cut in the
book is a quaint representation of the City Fathers of Barcelona
discussing naval regulations and maritime law (Fig. 90). This
is the first edition in Castilian (there were earlier ones in Catalan)
of a book which was the foundation of all modern laws relating to the sea. The *Disputatio de armis clericorum*, of Jaime
Montanyans, in 1536, has a good title-page in red and black,

with a border of separate compartment cuts.   Another rare example from this press, which appeared in 1531, is the *Libre de consells* of Jaime Roig.   The book is a bitter satire upon women, written in verse, and this first edition is very rare, Salvá stating

FIG. 91.—F. Garrido de Villena—*El verdadero sucesso de la famosa batalla de Roncesualles*, Valencia, Joan Mey Flandro, 1555.

that he had only seen two perfect copies.   On the recto of the last leaf there is a full-page cut representing the Virgin enthroned with the Child in her arms and St. Dorothea and St. Eulalia standing on each side of her.   The cut is signed " H."

Pedro de Huete established a press in Valencia shortly after the middle of the century.   A *Psalterium* of Bonaventura, which he printed in 1570, is pleasingly executed in red and black. On the title-page the Saint is depicted kneeling in adoration before a crucifix, and on the verso there is a conventional representation of the Virgin and Child. Another of his books, the *Libro de Reloges Solares* of Pedro Roiz, which he printed in 1575, is a scientific treatise with many cuts and diagrams and an alphabet of well-designed capitals. One of the rarest of the Valencian illustrated books of the sixteenth century, is *El verdadero sucesso de la famosa batalla de Roncesualles* of Francisco Garrido de Villena, printed by Joan de Mey Flandro in 1555. In addition to a woodcut portrait of the author (Fig. 91), the book has a series of cuts of Italian design and character which are not without merit.

FIG. 92.—Device of Pablo Hurus used in the fifteenth century.

FIG. 93.—Marineus—*De primis Aragoniae regibus*, Zaragoza, G. Coci, 1509.
(Device of Coci.)

CHAPTER VIII.

ZARAGOZA AND THE WORK OF COCI.

ZARAGOZA in the sixteenth century, so far as illustrated books are concerned, is chiefly notable for the work of one of Spain's greatest printers, Georg Coci. He was a German, and habitually describes himself as such in his colophons. He succeeded to the press of Pablo and Juan Hurus. He was responsible, as early as the years 1499 and 1500, for four books, which he printed in conjunction with Leonardo Hutz and Lupo Appentegger. Of these books, two are illustrated, the only one we need mention being the *Officia Quotidiana*, produced on 30th July, 1500 (Haebler, 490). An extremely rare book, it contains numerous cuts representing scenes in the life of Christ, besides figures of the Apostles and some Fathers of the Church. All these books were printed with the types and the device of Pablo Hurus, and it is not until about 1506 that we find Coci striking out on his own account. In 1508, he is responsible for the first edition which has survived of that world-famous romance of chivalry, *Amadis de Gaula* (*los quatro libros de*). Of this edition, only one copy has survived. It was found in Ferrara in 1872, and was sold to Baron Seillière for 10,000 francs. It passed, at the disposal of his library, into the hands of Quaritch, and thereafter found a final resting-place in our own National Library. The title-page of the book has a large and imposing cut of a Knight on horseback,[1] besides a number of decorative woodcut capital letters throughout the text.

It is impossible within the limits of space at our disposal,

---

[1] For a reproduction, see Sanchez, *Bibliografia Zaragozana* (No. 26).

to do more than draw attention to some of the outstanding examples of Coci's illustrated books. Anyone desirous of investigating the output from his press in any detail, will find much available material in the first volume of the bibliography of Zaragoza books in the sixteenth century, written by Sr. J. M. Sanchez, whose own fine collection of books was dispersed, under very disadvantageous circumstances during the years of the War. In 1509, Coci produced the *De primis Aragoniae regibus* of Lucius Marineus. The title-page has a cut which represents an angel holding up a shield, within which are the Arms of Aragon. This cut is also to be found in the *Coronica de Aragon*, printed by Pablo Hurus in 1498.[1]

At the end of the *De primis Aragoniae regibus* is the device of Coci, an adaptation of the Hurus mark, but instead of the triangles in the centre (Fig. 92), the initials of Coci now appear with his own motto (taken from Eccles., cap. vi.) substituted ; the Saints on each side being the same, viz. St. Roch and St. Sebastian (Fig. 93). There are a number of cuts in the book, mostly portraits of Kings, with scroll work extending down the inner margin of the page. One of the most striking of these portrait cuts appears on fol. xviii b, and represents Raimundus and his fiancée, Petronilla. An edition of the *Carcel de amor* of San Pedro, in 1511, has some cuts, while a later one of 1523, also printed by Coci, has an interesting title-page (Fig. 94) and a series of cuts throughout the text.

One of the rarest collections of ballads in the Spanish language is the *Cancionero de todas las obras de Iuan del enzina,* an edition of which Coci printed in 1516. It will be seen that the title-page has a well-designed woodcut of the Arms of the Catholic Kings (Fig. 95), which cut had been used by Pablo Hurus in his *Valerio Maximo* of 1495 (Haebler, 663). The second edition of this work appeared in Salamanca from the second anonymous press in 1496 (Haebler, 240).

[1] For reproduction, see Haebler, *Early Printers of Spain and Portugal* (Pl. XVIII.).

An entirely unrecorded edition of Fernando de Pulgar's *Los claros varones despaña*, which I acquired from the Fairfax Murray collection, presents an interesting example of Coci's work about 1510.   In the Fairfax Murray Sale in 1918, it was

C Carcel de amoz Compuesto poz
Diego de sant Pedro a pedimiēto del señoz
don Diego hernandez alcayde delos donze
les z de otros caualleros coztesanos: Nueua
mente histoziados y bien cozreydo.

FIG. 94.—San Pedro—*Carcel de amor*, Zaragoza, G. Coci, 1523.

catalogued as from an unidentified press.   Above the words of the title there is a cut (97 × 70 mm.), in which a man is shown sitting and writing at a desk, on which are pens, inkhorn and an hour-glass.   There is also a bookcase in the room, and from the window there is a view of a city set upon a hill.   On the side of the bookcase, in shadow, I found the well-known cypher of

Coci. The cut is within a border, the whole measuring 143 × 92 mm. (Fig. 96). I subsequently found this cut and the same border in the *Virgil* which Coci printed in 1513, a book of considerable rarity of which very few copies exist, one being

Cancionero de todas las
obras de Juan del enzina:con otras co-
fas nueuamente añadidas.·.

FIG. 95.—Juan de Enzina—*Cancionero*, Zaragoza, G. Coci, 1516.
(Reduced, original 228 × 137 mm.)

in the British Museum (*C. 56, d. 2*). This edition of *Los claros varones* contains biographies and letters of famous Spaniards. The author was Chronicler to Ferdinand and Isabella. This is apparently the earliest edition of the work in the sixteenth century. In 1518, we find the cut again in Petrarch's *De los remedios contra prospera y adversa fortuna*, but it is now surrounded by a large and elaborate compartment border, which also bears the cypher of Coci.

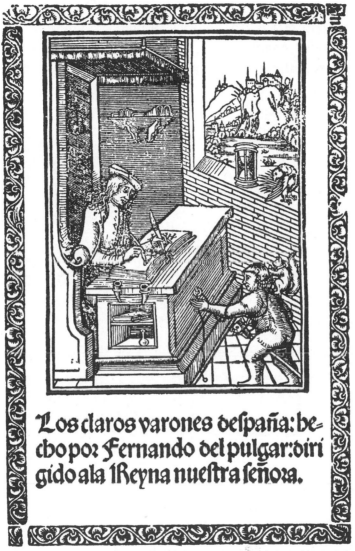

FIG. 96.—Pulgar—*Los claros varones despaña* [Zaragoza, G. Coci, *c.* 1510].

The year 1520 was notable for two productions from this press of outstanding interest from the point of view of their illustrations.   The first was the *Aurea expositio hymnorum* of Nebrissensis (Kal. Jan.), and the second, *Las quatorze decadas* of Livy

(24th May).   The *Aurea expositio hymnorum* has twenty-four
striking cuts, besides the device of the printer on the last leaf.
The cuts are by more than one hand, and while some of them
may be of the sixteenth century, others are undoubtedly of the
fifteenth.   For example, the full-page cut on the verso of the
title, depicting the vision of glory by St. Francis, appeared in the
first edition of the work printed by Pablo Hurus in 1492
(Haebler, 250(8)).   It is found again in another edition by the

FIG. 97.—Nebrissensis—*Aurea expositio hymnorum*, Zaragoza, G. Coci, 1520.

same printer in 1502.   The cut of the Resurrection, which is
found on fol. e5 of this 1520 edition, was also used by Hurus
for the same book in 1499 (Haebler, 76).   The rest of the cuts
in the book deal *inter alia* with scenes of the Passion, including
Christ before Pilate ; the Scourging (Fig. 26) ; the Carrying of
the Cross ; the Babe in the Manger, a remarkable cut (Fig. 97) ;
the Ascension ; the Martyrdom of St. Agatha ; the Birth of
John the Baptist, which shows his mother, Elizabeth, in bed ;
St. Martin ; St. Peter with the keys, etc.   The title-page of

this book is the same as in an edition which Haebler (255(5)) places *c*. 1500 and Sanchez in 1498. The first two lines of this title are xylographic, the remaining three being in ordinary type of a similar size. This book is a good illustration of the

FIG. 98.—Livy—*Las quatorze decadas*, Zaragoza, G. Coci, 1520.

use of the same woodcuts by different printers over a long number of years. There is no copy of this particular edition in the British Museum, but there is one in the Biblioteca Nacional at Madrid, another which came from the Sanchez collection, and the one in the writer's possession.

The very marked German influence on the book illustration
of the Coci press, is conspicuously evidenced in *Las quatorze
decadas* of Livy, printed in 1520.   A substantial and imposing
folio volume of upwards of 500 leaves, it is one of the most
finely printed books of the period.   The title-page affords an
example of colour printing, a large cut of the Royal Arms appearing in green, yellow and red.   On the verso of this title

FIG. 99.—Livy—*Las quatorze decadas*, Zaragoza, G. Coci, 1520.
(Device of Coci.)

there is a large full-page cut representing the enthronement of
Maximilian I., Emperor of the Romans.   Throughout the book
there are a large number of spirited half-page cuts, all of which
are taken from the same blocks which were used in an edition
in German, printed by J. Schoeffer in 1505 at Mainz.   The
cuts are well designed and contain considerable detail (Fig. 98).
The colophon leaf, which is a really beautiful piece of decorative
work and is printed in red and black, has a variation of Coci's

device.   The lions at the foot of it are now shown lying side by side in friendly companionship, as opposed to their mutually antagonistic appearance in the earlier states of this device (Figs. 99 and 100).   Some of the cuts in this book appeared later on in an edition of Pulgar's *Chronica de los Reyes Catholicos*, printed by Iuan Millan in this town in 1557.   An example is here repro-

FIG. 100.—Nebrissensis—*Aurea expositio hymnorum*, Zaragoza, G. Coci, 1520.
(Device of Coci, as used in this book, but without the border.)

duced (Fig. 101).   This edition of Livy is rarely found in perfect condition, the coloured title-page being generally missing.

Attention may now be called to what is perhaps one of the most interesting illustrated books printed in Spain at this period.   It is the *Flos Sanctorum* of Pedro de la Vega, who was the translator of the Livy.   The book is in two parts, the first consisting of a life of Christ and some of the Saints, while the second part gives more lives of Saints, and also those of the Apostles and Martyrs, each being placed under the appropriate

month in the calendar.   As far as I have been able to trace, the
first edition of this book was printed *c.* 1521, and a second one
in 1544, both from Coci's press.   The colophon of the 1544
edition reads : " Imprimido en casa del muy virtuoso varon
George Coci aleman : y a espensas de Pedro Bernuz, y Bartholome de Nagera : en la muy noble y imperial ciudad de Çaragoça.

FIG. 101.—Livy—*Las quatorze decadas*, Zaragoza, G. Coci, 1520.
Also,
Pulgar—*Chronica de los Reyes Catholicos*, Zaragoza, Juan Millan, 1567.
(Reduced, originals 119 × 145 mm.)

A cinco dias del mes de Deziembre, en el año del señor de mil
y quiniētos y quarenta y quatro."   This colophon is followed by
Coci's device, printed in red and black, from the same block as
used in the Livy of 1520.   The earlier edition of *c.* 1521 may
possibly have only comprised the first part of the book, as my
copy, which is apparently the only one which has survived, ends
without any printer's colophon, but with the following state-

ment : " Esta es la ultima capitulacion deste libro : que hizo fray Pedro/de la vega : de la orden del glorioso señor sant Hieronymo. Començo esta/obra en el monesterio de la bienavanturada virgen y martyr/santa Engracia de la noble ciudad de Çaragoça/del reyno de Aragō : y concluyola y /diole fin en el suso dicho mona-/sterio a xxv dias de Sep/tēbre año del señor de mil y / D xx, y/uno I.H.S.   MARIA." This copy was formerly in the Royal Library of Carlos I., King of Portugal, and bears his crowned cypher on the flyleaf. It will be remembered that Carlos I. and his son, the Crown Prince, were assassinated in the streets of Lisbon on the 1st of February, 1908.

The 1544 edition has the same statement at the end of the first part, but with the following addition : " y fue este libro quāto a su p̄mcra parte reconoscido emē/dado otra vez, y en muchas cosas añadido por el mismo/ autor en el suso dicho monesterio en el año/de Mil y quinientos y qua/renta y uno."

There is also a note on the verso of the title of the 1544 edition, to the effect that more than twenty years having elapsed since the book was printed, it was now revised because of printer's errors and sundry statements which had been found to require correction. That there were also certain additions, for example, the festivals of Lent, the Octave of Easter and specially, a life of St. Roch. The colophon at the end of the 1544 edition is clearly limited to the second part of the book and runs as follows : " A gloria y honra de la santissima y incomutable trinidad : y a/ ensalcamiento de los sacratissimos mysterios de nuestra santa fe catholica : y a venera/cion de la gloriosa virgen Maria nr̄a señora : y de todos los ciudadanos de la corte/ del cielo : aqui se acaba la segunda parte de libro que es llamado vida de Jesu/christo y de sus santos : segun la ultima y postrimera copilacion he-/cha por fray Pedro de la vega de la orden del glorioso señor / sant Hieronymo. Ha se imprimido en casa del muy/virtuoso varon George Coci aleman : y a / espensas de

Pedro Bernuz, y/ Bartholome de Nagera : /en la muy noble y Imperial ciudad de /çaragoça./   A cinco dias del mes de/Deziembre : en el/año del señor de/mil y quiniē/ tos y qua/renta y /qua/tro./ "

This is all printed in red and Coci's device is at the foot. Nicholas Antonio, in his account of Pedro de Vega (*Bibliotheca Nova*, vol. ii., p. 246), says there was an edition of the book in 1521 or 1522, and the title he gives corresponds with the earlier edition, which I date as *c.* 1521, viz. :—" Flos Sanctorum. /La vida de nr̄o señor iesu cristo/y de su sct' issima madre:y d'los otros S̄cos : segū la ordē de sus fiestas./ "

The 1544 edition, containing both parts of the book, omits the words " Flos Sanctorum " which form the first line of the title in the earlier edition.   As the author speaks of the more than twenty years which have elapsed since he first entrusted it to the printer, we may reasonably assume that we have here the first and second editions of this work, and that although originally it may have been intended to issue the second part with the earlier edition, such second part was not in fact actually printed until 1544.

J. M. Sanchez, who we may assume had as good opportunities of tracing editions of Zaragoza books as anyone, cannot give a description of any edition from any copy he has seen. Under the year 1520, he attributes a *Vida de cristo* to Pedra de la Vega, based on an alleged entry in the catalogue of Gabriel Soro.   It is quite clear that this is an error, as we learn from Vega himself that he only finished writing the first part in September, 1521.   Under the year 1521, he quotes Antonio and says he has never seen an edition of either 1521 or 1522. Under the year 1544, he gives a partial and imperfect description of the edition of that year, which he has taken from the catalogue of Jose María Nepomuceno, printed in Lisbon in 1897.   The only other edition mentioned by Sanchez is under the year 1548, where he copies an entry from the catalogue (1895, No. 148) of Quaritch, relating to an edition printed by Bartholome Nagera in Zaragoza in 1548, which

FIG. 102.—Pedro de la Vega—*Flos Sanctorum*, Zaragoza, G. Coci, *c.* 1521.
(Reduced, original 319 × 217 mm., and printed in colours.)

edition contained 458 leaves, the copy in question lacking all the leaves from 1 to 226. Quaritch describes it as the first edition and added: "This original edition is so rare as to be unknown to Gallardo and Salvá!" As a matter of fact, Gallardo (No. 4207) can only describe an edition printed by J. Gutierrez in Seville in 1572, which is also the only edition of the book in the British Museum (487, 1. 4). Salvá can only refer to Pedro de la Vega as the translator of the Livy of 1520. Latassa mentions the work, and cites an edition printed at Zaragoza in 1525, but needless to say can give no particulars.[1]

I have dealt at some length with the bibliographical side of these two early editions, because the book is not only profusely illustrated with a large number of remarkable wood-cuts, but its title-page presents, as far as I know, the first example in Spain of colour printing in as many as five different colours. The words of the title are printed in red, the whole page being enclosed with a compartment border, the subjects including children and fruit, Fathers and dignitaries of the Church, with the interiors of ecclesiastical buildings, etc. One small cut in this border which is twice repeated, depicts a Cardinal's hat, under which a lion is reposing on the ground. The words "Cū privilegio imperiali" appear at the foot in the earlier edition, but are left out in 1544. The centre of the page, above the words of the title, is occupied by a large cut showing a tree springing out of a red rose, being emblematical of our Lord and His Saints. The central figure of Christ has been left uncoloured in the earlier edition, but the rest of the cut is printed in five colours, viz. :—red, dark brown, yellow, blue, and a light brown, tinged with green, is used for the foliage of the tree (see Frontispiece). A reproduction of the whole title-page, reduced in size, will indicate the character of the work (Fig. 102).

[1] Fernandez in his *Impresos de Alcalá en la Biblioteca del Escorial* (Madrid, 1913), gives a description from an imperfect copy of an Alcalá Edition of 1556, revised and edited "por fray Martin de lilio de la orden de San Francisco."

In the earlier edition the verso of the title-page is occupied by a full-page cut of the Crucifixion, with a considerable number of figures in the foreground and some castellated buildings on the hills in the distance. This cut is from the same block which was used by Pablo Hurus in his *Breidenbach*, in 1498. H. W. Davies describes it as " a masterly design, the modelling of one of the horses being excellent, the fainting figure of Mary, the mother of Christ, finely and naturally represented, and the draperies carefully studied and arranged." The cut is typically Spanish in character and treatment, and there is little doubt that it is the work of a native craftsman. It does not appear in the 1544 edition, its place being taken by an uncoloured print of the centre cut from the title, but within a different compartment border. On the verso of fol. v, there is a cut of the Resurrection, obviously a copy on a reduced scale of one which appears in Schedel's *Nuremberg Chronicle*, printed by Koberger at Nuremberg in 1493 (Fig. 103). This copy is first to be found in the *Donatus* of 1498, printed by Fadrique de Basilea at Burgos. The remainder of the cuts in the earlier edition of the book are of very special interest. As they, and many others, are to be found in the 1544 edition (which contains both parts of the work), the descriptions and references which follow relate to that edition. In addition to the coloured title-page, the book contains some 192 cuts. Of these, no fewer than 154 are oblong cuts running across the page, and of an average measurement of 89 × 187 mm. All these are from the original blocks used in the *Passional* of Jacobus de Voragine, printed by Koberger at Nuremberg on 5th December, 1488 (B.M., I.C. 7400). A typical example of these cuts, representing the murder of St. Thomas à Becket, is here reproduced (Fig. 104). Attention may also be directed to the cut which represents the birth of John the Baptist, with a view of a kitchen and the nurse holding the child, sitting with her feet in a tub of water (Fig. 105). Later on in the book it does duty again to represent the birth of the Virgin Mary ! The

cuts include some interesting subjects, including the studio of
St. Luke, with a boy engaged in mixing colours ; St. Clara in

Juſtus es domine:⁊ rectum iudicium tuũ.

FIG. 103.—Donatus—*De octo partibus orationis*, Burgos, Fadrique de Basilea, 1498.
Also,
Pedro de la Vega—*Flos Sanctorum*, Zaragoza, G. Coci, *c.* 1521.

adoration before the monstrance ; St. Benedict and some monks
in a refectory ; The Annunciation ; and Eustachio and his com-

panions in a hunting scene. In the 1488 *Passional* there is a
large cut on the first leaf of the text (178 × 180 mm.) which
shows St. Ambrose sitting on a throne, with two dogs in the
foreground, and a scribe seated and writing, while a crowd of
officials and others are seen in the background. This cut

FIG. 104.—Pedro de la Vega—*Flos Sanctorum*, Zaragoza, G. Coci, *c.* 1521.

appears here on fol. ccxxi, and is used to illustrate the life of
St. Isidore, Archbishop of Seville (Fig. 106).

A similar large cut of St. Michael, engaged in weighing a
nude figure in scales, presumably a human soul, against two
devils, with a group of clergy bearing processional crosses in the
background, figures in both books.

The smaller cuts in the book mainly depict incidents in
the life of Christ. Several of them are adaptations from the

"Delbecq-Schreiber Passion," and had already appeared in the *Tesoro de la pasion* of Andres de Li in 1494, and again in the Spanish *Breidenbach* of 1498 (see p. 38).   The remainder of the small cuts are mainly of Spanish workmanship, most of them having also appeared in the *Breidenbach*, while others are clearly copies from the *Voragine*, printed by M. Huss at Lyons in 1486.

FIG. 105.—Pedro de la Vega—*Flos Sanctorum*, Zaragoza, G. Coci, 1544.

One of the most interesting of these represents St. George and the Dragon.   A typical cut from the Coci press, and one of the smallest in the book (50 × 49 mm.), appears on fol. cxxx, and shows two angels upholding the monstrance.   This cut can be found again in the *Oficio del Corpus*, which Coci printed in 1529, a book which Sanchez (No. 155) describes as one of the extraordinary rare productions of the Zaragoza press in the sixteenth century, it being the first edition printed in Spain of this particular liturgical work.

FIG. 106.—Pedro de la Vega—*Flos Sanctorum*, Zaragoza, G. Coci, 1544.

Both the editions of the *Flos Sanctorum* are finely printed in red and black, in Gothic type, and in addition to the cuts, contain alphabets of well-designed woodcut capitals.   The book affords a conspicuous example of fine book production from this press, in respect of press work, decoration and illustration.   The extreme rarity of these two editions (I know of no other copies than those in my possession) is no doubt due to their illustrations having made them one of the popular picture books of the period, with a consequent liability to destruction by constant wear and tear.   Apart from the illustrations, the text provides details and particulars of the lives of Spanish Saints and Martyrs, which are not found elsewhere.

Pedro Bernuz and Bartholome de Nagera were the next two printers to maintain the traditions of the Coci press.   Their names appear, after the death of Coci (which, according to Sanchez, took place in 1546) in some cases as publishers, and in other cases as the actual printers of books which appeared about that time.   Their partnership did not last very long, and we find them later on engaged with separate and distinct presses.   The *Missale Romanum* of 1548, which has Coci's name in the colophon and his device, bears their monogram and small device in the lower compartment border of the title-page, which also has a large cut of St. Jerome and the lion, after Durer.   This Missal is beautifully printed in red and black, the music being on a four-line stave.   There are several full-page cuts within compartment borders, some of them being from the same blocks used in the *Breidenbach* of 1498 and later in the *Flos Sanctorum* of *c.* 1521.   Sanchez can only record two copies of this book, his own and one in the Biblioteca Nacional at Madrid.   The reproduction of one of the cuts given here (Fig. 107) is from a copy of the book formerly in the collection of the late George Dunn, of Wooley Hall, and now in my possession.

A rare little *Procesionario Cisterciense*, of 1550, printed by Pedro Bernuz, has another of the cuts which appeared in the

Breidenbach of 1498. It appears on the verso of the title and represents the Presentation in the Temple. The *Evangelios* of Ambrosio Montesino, printed by Bartholome de Nagera in 1555,

Maria auté cóferuabat omnia verba bec cóferens in cozde suo. Et reuersi sunt pasto res glozificátes z laudátes deñ.zc.Luce.2.

FIG. 107.—*Missale Romanum*, Zaragoza, G. Coci, 1548.
(The words in original are printed in red.)

has some decorative woodcut initials, but lacks the illustrations, which we shall see later, were so conspicuous a feature of an earlier edition printed in Toledo.

FIG. 108.—Juan de Iciar—*Arte breve y provechoso de cuenta Castellana y Arithmetica.* Zaragoza, Miguel de Çapila, 1559.

No consideration of the illustrated books of Zaragoza in the sixteenth century would be complete without reference to the works of Juan de Iciar, which were published in the middle of the century. Designed to teach the arts of writing and arithmetic, they were copiously illustrated with ornamental alphabets, full-page emblematic figures, specimens of calligraphy,

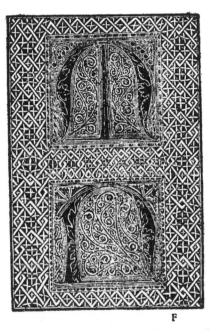

FIG. 109.—Juan de Iciar—*Arte breve y provechoso de cuenta Castellana y Arithmetica*, Zaragoza, Miguel de Çapila, 1559.
(Reduced, original 156 × 104 mm.)

some of them on black backgrounds, and many of them dated by the author in various years between 1547 and 1550. A woodcut portrait of Iciar by Juan de Vingles, which is found in most of the editions, is reproduced here from the *Arte Breve y provechoso de cuenta Castellana y Arithmetica*, which was published " en casa de Miguel de çapila " in 1559 (Fig. 108). A typical example of the ornamental alphabets from the same book is also reproduced (Fig. 109). Juan de Vingles, the engraver, who collaborated with Iciar, is described by Rufino Blanco,[1] as "grabador zaragozano," while Stirling Maxwell, in the *Annals of the Artists of Spain*, calls him a Frenchman. Whatever may

FIG. 110.—G. Montemayor—*Diana*, Zaragoza, Viuda de B. de Nagera, 1570.

have been his nationality, he affords one of the few instances in early Spanish books of the craftsman who habitually signed his work in full, or by initials. Iciar laid Italian, German and

[1] Rufino Blanco, *Diccionario Caligrafos Españoles*.

Flemish writers under contribution for many of his ideas and designs, and produced in these books instruction in calligraphy, which for many years in Spain remained unequalled in quality

SIGVESE LA EXPLI-
cació del Motu Proprio de Pio
Quinto, que trata de los cenfos,
conforme lo que fe guarda en
eftos Reynos, con algunas
aduertencias y dudas
Prouechofas.

EN ÇARAGOÇA,
En cafa de Pedro Puig, año. 1591.

FIG. 111.—M. Rodriguez—*Explicacion de la Bulla de la Sancta Cruzada*, Zaragoza, Pedro Puig, 1591.

or extent. Complete copies of his books are practically not to be found to-day, as like all early books for students, they were speedily thumbed out of existence.

The widow of Bartholome de Nagera was responsible, in

1570, for the *Primera aedicion de los siete libros de la Diana de George Montemayor*, of which Sanchez says the only known copy is an imperfect one in the Biblioteca Nacional at Madrid. The reproduction of the title-page, with the woodcut representations of Diana, Sireus and Sylvano (Fig. 110), is taken from a perfect copy in my collection.

Pedro Puig produced in 1591 and 1592 an *Explicacion de la Bulla de la Sancta Crusada*, written by Manuel Rodriguez, which has a neat cut on the title of the last tract in the book, which shows two angels holding up the monstrance, a new design of a subject which often occupied the attention of the earlier Zaragoza woodcutters. The cut, which is here reproduced, is from the only recorded copy, formerly in the library of Jacques Auguste De Thou (1553-1617) and afterwards in the Britwell Court collection, from whence it was acquired by the writer (Fig. 111). If we except a magnificently printed and decorated *Antiphonarium*, produced in 1598, " Ex Typographia Paschalis Perez," the history of the printing press in Zaragoza during the last quarter of the century, is characterised by obvious deterioration in press work, and an almost entire absence of any artistic merit in decoration, or illustration.

CHAPTER IX.

BARCELONA.

In dealing with the printing press in Barcelona in the fifteenth century, some of the prominent printers overlapped into the fol-

Carta dela grã victoria

y presa de Oran. Enla qual se contiene la for

ma y manera de como es estada ganada Con vnas que dizen la misma victoria. Con dos villãçetes por muy gentil estilo.

FIG. 112.—*Carta de la grã victoria y presa de Oran* [Barcelona, Carlos Amoros, *c.* 1509].

lowing one, and their later work has already been mentioned. Pedro Posa, Juan Rosembach and Juan Luschner are cases in point. The first printer whose work actually commenced in the sixteenth

(147)

century was Carlos Amoros. One of his early productions was a *Carta de la grā victoria y presa de Oran*, being a contemporary account of the siege and capture of Oran from the Moors in 1509.[1] On the title of this tract there is a cut, which he also used to illustrate the destruction of Jerusalem by Titus, A.D. 70 (Fig. 112). This account of the siege of Oran has apparently survived in only two copies, one is in the collection of the Duque

FIG. 113.—*Privilegia Fratrum Minorum*, Barcelona, Carlos Amoros, 1523.
(Reduced, original 167 × 137 mm.)

de Medinaceli, and the other was acquired by the writer in Barcelona. In 1518, Amoros produced an edition of the *Consolat de mar*, which has a few cuts, one of which represents the Virgin and Child, with an "oratio pro navigantibus." The *Privilegia Fratrum Minorum*, printed in 1523, is an interesting book in three parts, the first two having separate woodcut title-

[1] For particulars of the siege of Oran, see the Author's *Cardinal Ximenes*, London, 1917.

FIG. 114.—*Tragicomedia de Calisto y Melibea*, Barcelona, Carlos Amoros, 1525.

pages, on the verso of each of which there is a striking xylo-graphic cut with letterpress and figures of our Lord, the Pope and St. Francis, giving rules to the twelve monks, the whole within four woodcut borders in the side margins (Fig. 113). This particular book, dealing with the Order of St. Francis, is of some rarity.   The copy in the British Museum contains only two of the parts.   The writer's copy, containing all three parts,

FIG. 115.—Pere Miguel Carbonell—*Croniques de Espāya*, Barcelona, Carlos Amoros, 1546.

has a MS. verification of the text by the Public Notary of Bar-celona.

Two years later, in 1525, one of the early and extremely rare editions of *La Celestina* was issued from this press.   In addition to the woodcut title-page, which we are able to reproduce from the only surviving copy (formerly in the Miró collection) (Fig. 114), there are twenty-three other cuts representing actors and scenes in the play.   Of these, the one depicting the death of

Celestina, is an interesting example of the work of the period (fol. vi verso). Amoros was also responsible for the first edition of *Las Obras de Boscan*, in 1543, with a decorative and well-designed title-page.

The last work of Amoros to which attention may be called is the *Croniques de Espāya* of Pere Miquel Carbonell (1546),

FIG. 116.—Pere Miquel Carbonell—*Croniques de Espāya*, Barcelona, Carlos Amoros, 1546.
(Device of printer.)

which in addition to a decorative woodcut title-page, has some cuts, one of which is here reproduced (Fig. 115), as well as the device of the printer (Fig. 116).

Pedro Botin, a Barcelona printer of whom little is known, was responsible in 1550 for a remarkable and extremely scarce book of Gundisalvus de Sojo, entitled *Historia y Milagros de nuestra Señora de Montserrat*, which he brought out for Pedro

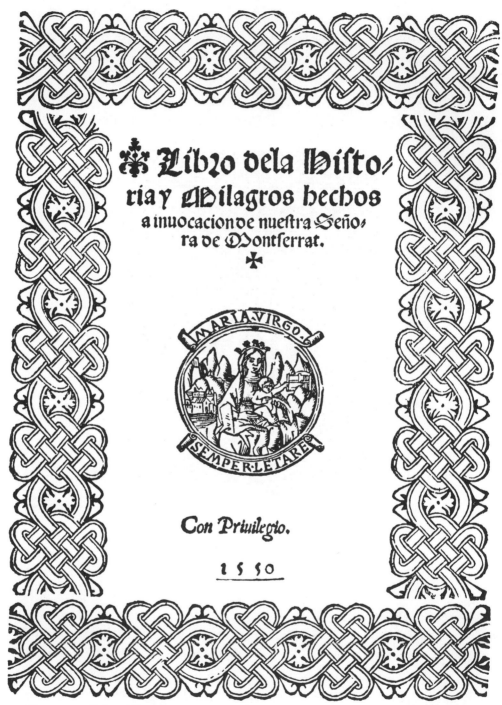

FIG. 117.—Sojo—*Historia y Milagros de nuestra Señora de Montserrat*, Barcelona, Pedro Mompezat, 1550.

Mompezat, another printer in the town. The book is remarkable for the specially fine woodcut border on the title (Fig. 117), also for a cut of the Virgin and Child, with the mountain in the background, a close copy of a cut used many years earlier by Juan Rosembach, both at Montserrat and Barcelona. This cut is now found within striking outline compartment borders, and the book is decorated throughout with a series of historiated and other woodcut capitals. The copy in the possession of the writer was formerly in the collection of Heber, Richard Ford and Huth,

FIG. 118.—Diego Gracian—*De re militari*, Barcelona, Claudio Bornat, 1567. (Device of printer.)

and is of exceptional association interest. Richard Ford, in the first edition of his famous *Handbook of Spain*, 1845, refers to his ownership of this copy, in the flyleaf of which he has made a long signed memorandum, in which he alludes to the fact that Charles V. ascended the mountain in July, 1551. On another flyleaf there is an autograph inscription by T. Von Freundtsperg, the Commander of Charles V.'s *German Hansknechts*, to the effect that he purchased the book on the mountain itself (at the Monastery ?) on 23rd July, 1551. Ford complains of the " booby country binder," who had cut out the flyleaf with this note, but adds that he had had it bound in again, and that "this rare book was purchased by me at Heber's Sale." There is no copy in the British Museum, and the only copy, other than the writer's, is in private hands in Barcelona.

SILVA DE
VARIOS RO-
MANCES RECOPI-
lados, y con diligencia efcogidos
los mejores Romáces de
los tres libros dela
Silua.

*Y agora nueuamente añadidos cinco Ro-
mances dela armada dela Liga, y quatro
dela fentécia de don Albaro de Luna, y no
del cerco de Malta, y otro dela mañana
de fant Iuan, otro mira Nero
de Tarpeya y otros
muchos.*

Impreſſa en Barcelona
en caſa de Hubert Gotard.
Año. 1587.
A coſta de Onofre Gori.

FIG. 119.—*Silva de varios Romances*, Barcelona, Hubert Gotard, 1587.

Claudio Bornat was responsible about this time for several well-printed and decorated books, including the *De re militari* of Diego Gracian, from which is reproduced his device (Fig. 118).

Among the old Spanish ballad books which have survived, a collection known as *Silva de varios Romances*, printed in Barcelona by Hubert Gotard in 1587, is of considerable rarity. From the reproduction of the title-page (Fig. 119), it will be seen how much the decoration of the printed page had deteriorated in Barcelona towards the end of the century, a deterioration which we have already noted in Zaragoza, and which was also to be seen in many other towns at this period. There is no copy of this edition of the *Silva de varios Romances* in the British Museum, but they have copies of the editions containing only the first part, which were printed both at Zaragoza and Barcelona in 1550.

In leaving the illustrated books at Barcelona in the sixteenth century, we can but pay tribute to the artistic skill, energy and originality with which her two outstanding printers, Juan Rosembach and Carlos Amoros, laboured over a long period of years to produce books of special merit in regard to their decoration and illustration.

𝕿ragicomedia de Calisto y Meli
bea: enla qual se contiene de mas
de su agradable τ dulce estilo mu,
chas sentencias filosofales: τ aui,
sos muy necessarios para mance,
bos: mostrandoles los engaños ꝗ
estan encerrados en seruientes τ
alcabuetas: τ nueuamente añadi,
do el tractado de Centurio.

FIG. 120.—*Tragicomedia de Calisto y Melibea* [Seville, 1502 (?)].

CHAPTER X.

SEVILLE AND THE WORK OF THE CROM-BERGERS.

THE absence of any really reliable bibliography of the books printed at Seville is much to be regretted. The *Tipografía Hispalense* of Francisco Escudero y Perosso (Madrid, 1894), is in many respects incomplete and sometimes inaccurate, but to his pioneer work we owe the only attempt that has been made, however imperfectly, to bring together any considerable information on the output of books at this town in the sixteenth century.

The printers in the town were numerous, at least fifty can be traced during this century, but as is so often the case, the number of those whose work deserves any detailed examination is very strictly limited. The names of Jacobo and Juan Cromberger, the greatest printers in many respects in all Spain during this period, will always reflect honour on the town of Seville. It is generally accepted that they were father and son, and that Jacobo was a German. He alludes to his nationality over and over again in the colophons of his books. Juan Cromberger, on the other hand, is never so described, and it is fairly safe to assume that his mother was a Spanish lady. A very interesting account of the Cromberger family and their activities is given by Haebler,[1] who rightly draws attention to the large proportion of their books which consist of *belles lettres*, including some of the most famous of the romances of chivalry.

According to Dr. Burger, the first book printed by Jacobo Cromberger was an edition of *La Celestina* in 1502, and he cites

---

[1] Haebler, *The Early Printers of Spain and Portugal*, London, 1897 (pp. 55-67).

(157)

Escudero (No. 121) as his authority. This edition has only survived, as far as I know, in two copies, one in the British Museum and one in my own collection. The British Museum copy lacks the last leaf, and has in its place an alleged colophon, with the date 1501 and the device of Polonus.

The whole of this leaf is a fake. The copy came from the Seillière collection and has always been regarded with suspicion, but until my copy afforded an opportunity for comparison, the true facts were uncertain. The book has a striking cut on the title (80 × 113 mm.) (Fig. 120), and in addition, there are twenty-three other cuts throughout the text.

The rhyming colophon on the last leaf alleges that the book was printed in Seville in 1502, but I have come to the conclusion that it is more likely to have been printed in Italy at a later date, probably between 1510 and 1515. I also think that the printers will be found to be Jacobo de Junta and Antonio de Salamanca, of Rome, who printed the 1525 edition of *Esplandian*, the well-known romance of chivalry, which forms the fifth book of the Amadis series. I am confirmed in my opinion by the fact that Alonso de Proaza, who was the corrector of the press in the *Celestina*, acted in a similar capacity in the *Esplandian*, and in other Spanish books printed in Rome at this period. Again, it is not without significance that in his address to his friend by the author on the verso of the title of the *Celestina*, we read, "a un *suo* amigo," the Italian *suo* being employed instead of the Spanish "su," a slip which was corrected in another Spanish edition printed at Venice in 1534. Further, my copy has been plentifully annotated in the margins in Italian in a contemporary hand. The illustrated books printed in Spanish, but outside Spain, afford considerable interest, and include many important books, as for example, the first edition of the *New Testament in Spanish* (Antwerp, 1543), but they are beyond the scope of the present work and must be left for separate and future treatment. We first find Jacobo Cromberger working

FIG. 121.—*Soror Lucia* [Seville, Jacobo Cromberger, y L. Polono, *c.* 1503].

as a printer at Seville in conjunction with Ladislao Polono, whose responsibility for the first book printed at Alcalá has already been mentioned.

In 1503, Cromberger and Polonus printed an edition of *La summa de confesion* of St. Antoninus of Florence, on the title of which there is a cut which represents a master and his pupil. It is about this period, or perhaps a little later, that I attribute to these printers, or to Cromberger alone, a very rare tract entitled, *Soror Lucia*, which bears no imprint or date, but which is undoubtedly printed with the early types of Cromberger. The striking cut on the title is here reproduced (Fig. 121).

In 1507, we find Cromberger working alone and producing an illustrated edition in quarto of *La Historia de Oliveros de Castilla y Artus de Algarve*, another edition of which, in folio, he printed in 1509. I have a copy of a small quarto volume, *Coplas de Mingo Revulgo glosadas por Fernado de pulgar*, which bears the following colophon : " Aqui se acaban las coplas del revulgo con su glosa : em/primidas en la muy noble y muy leal cibdad de Sevilla : /por Jacobo cronberguer (*sic*) aleman. Año de señor de mil y/quinientos y diez. a. x. dias de Febrero." On the title there is a cut (84 × 78 mm.) representing a left-handed man writing at a table, with an open book opposite him on a shelf (Fig. 122). This same cut was used by Jacobo Cromberger in his editions of Mendoza's *Proverbios*, in 1509 and 1526, and he used it again in Almella's *Valerio* of 1527. The cut and the words of the title are within a woodcut border, and on the verso of this leaf there is a fine decorative initial letter (40 × 40 mm.), white on a black background. At the end of my copy of this edition, the only one I have been able to trace, some verses are written in a contemporary Spanish hand. Commencing with some reflections on death, and with an invocation to the Virgin, a discussion follows which is alleged to have taken place between King Alexander and Aristotle, in which maxims are propounded such as :—

" Be benign to all, familiar to few and a flatterer to none."

" Be constant in adversity and humble and devout in prosperity."

" Do not engage in law with a more powerful adversary."

" Do not give away your secrets to a woman or a child."

FIG. 122.—Pulgar—*Coplas de Mingo Revulgo*, Seville, Jacobo Cromberger, 1510.

A good example of this printer's careful press-work and well-designed decorative woodcut capitals, is provided in the second Spanish edition of Petrarch's *De los remedios cōtra prospera*

y adversa fortuna which he published in February, 1513.   The
decoration of the title consists of a fine cut of the Arms of
Gonzalvo de Cordova (" el gran capitan "), to whom the translation is dedicated, and this is within borders of birds, foliage and
emblematic figures, which combine to present a pleasing and
well-proportioned page.

We now turn to one of Cromberger's early picture books,
which deserves more than passing mention.   It is an edition of
the *Retablo de la vida de cristo* of Juan de Padilla (1468-1518),
who was known as " the Carthusian."   The book, which appeared in 1518, consists of a long poem in octave stanzas, and
gives an account of the life of our Lord, as related by prophets
and evangelists.   It is profusely illustrated with upwards of eighty
interesting cuts.   The one on the title, taken from the same
block as used by Ungut and Polonus in 1492 (Haebler, 145), in
their edition of Cavalca's *Espejo de la cruz* (Fig. 48), is now
within an ornamental border.   The verso of the third leaf is
entirely occupied by no less than twenty compartment cuts,
which represent, *inter alia*, The Annunciation, The Nativity,
The Baptism of Christ, The Descent of the Holy Ghost,
The Crucifixion, The Resurrection, and various figures of Saints
and Fathers of the Church (Fig. 123).   The cuts throughout the
text, averaging 56 × 49 mm., illustrate scenes in the life of Christ.
On the recto of the last leaf there is a specially fine woodcut
portrait of John the Baptist, measuring 152 × 154 mm. and
which is here reproduced (Fig. 124).   This cut was used again
in 1521 by another Seville printer, Juan Varela of Salamanca, to
illustrate the same author's *Los doce triumphos de los doce apostolos*,
a book which takes its place among " Americana," on the
strength of a brief reference to Columbus in one of the triumphs.
This edition of the *Retablo de la vida de cristo* has hitherto been
unrecorded, and no doubt the edition of the same year, which
Nic. Antonio (followed by Escudero) has attributed to the press
of Juan Varela, is a mistake.   In any case, this Cromberger

FIG. 123.—Padilla—*Retablo de la vida de cristo*, Seville, Jacobo Cromberger, 1518.

INTER NATOS MVLIERVM NO SVREXIT MAIOR IOHANE BAPTISTA

¶ Esta diuina obra fue muy diligente mente examinada ⁊ aprouada por los reuerendos señores don Fernando dela torre dean dela sancta yglesia de Seuilla: ⁊ maestre Rodrigo de sancta ella canonigo enla dicha yglesia ⁊ arcediano de reyna: ⁊ maestre francisco frayle dela orden delos me nores: ⁊ otros doctos religiosos en presencia del auctor dela obra.

FIG. 124.—Padilla—*Retablo de la vida de cristo*, Seville, Jacobo Cromberger, 1518.

edition is of extreme rarity. My copy was formerly in the library of Alvaro Virgilio de Franco Teixeira, whose ex-libris bears the pleasing motto, " boni libri, boni amici."

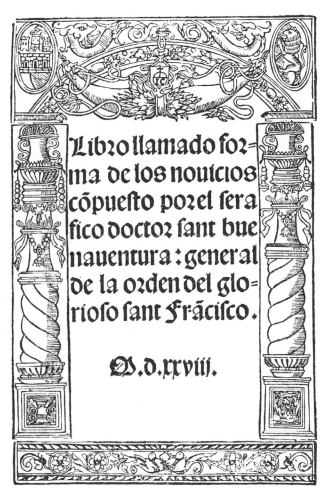

Fig. 125.—S. Bonaventura—*Forma de los novicios*, Seville, Jacobo Cromberger, 1528.
(Reduced, original 244 × 159 mm., and printed in red and black.)

The year 1528 was the last one in which we find Jacobo Cromberger printing by himself, and he signalised it by the second edition in Spanish of the *Illustres mugeres* of Boccaccio. With the exception of some crude cuts on the title, the book is without illustration, and in marked contrast to the fine first edition produced at the Hurus press in Zaragoza in the fifteenth century, to which reference has already been made (p. 33). Another book of this year was an edition of the *Forma de los novicios* of S. Bonaventura, which is cited without particulars by Escudero (No. 281), on the authority of a note made by Señor Gayangos. The reproduction of the title-page, in the top border of which will be found Cromberger's small device, is taken from a copy formerly in the Royal Library of Carlos I., King of Portugal (Fig. 125).

Between 1525 and 1528, Jacobo Cromberger is found associated with Juan Cromberger in the production of some nine or ten books, notably a *Celestina* of 1525 and the *Visio delectable* of Alfonso de la Torre in 1526, both of which contain cuts.

Juan Cromberger commenced to print by himself in 1528, and although he died in 1540, or thereabouts, his press continued for a long number of years after his death. To illustrate his work, we will give some examples. In the *Relox de principes* of Guevara, which he published in 1531, we have an example of a book which, without any cuts in the text, is nevertheless a fine specimen of a well-printed and decorated book. The title, printed in red and black, with a cut of the Royal Arms, is within heavy woodcut borders of emblematic and architectural design, giving to the whole page an imposing effect. Each of the three books included in the volume has a separate title-page, and as an example of the pleasing combination of type, decorative capital letters and well-designed borders, one of them is here reproduced (Fig. 126). It will be observed that the border is the same as used three years before, when father and son were working together, and the improvement in the composition of the page is apparent.[1]

In the same year (1531), in the fourth part of the *Vita*

[1] Cf. Fig. 125.

Christi Cartuxano of Ludophus de Saxonia, translated by Ambrosio Montesino, we have a full-page cut of the Crucifixion which is of special merit (Fig. 127).

FIG. 126.—Antonio de Guevara—*Relox de principes*, Seville, Juan Cromberger, 1531.
(Reduced, original 242 × 159 mm.)

There is also one on the title-page, depicting the Last Supper, which is not without interest. The recorded copy of this book is in the Biblioteca de Valencia, and the one in the writer's possession was another of the books formerly in the Royal Library of Carlos I., King of Portugal.

Attention has already been drawn to the catholicity of taste evinced by the Cromberger press in the literary contents of their books.   An illustration of this is afforded in the edition of *Los quatro libros de Amadis de gaula*, which Juan Cromberger produced in 1535.   An imposing folio volume, the words of the title are printed in red below a fine woodcut equestrian portrait of a knight, with his attendants and a view of castellated buildings in the background, the whole being within woodcut borders (Fig. 128).   This cut, with some slight variations, appeared in the 1531 edition of the same work and has been reproduced by Salvá (vol. ii., p. 5).   Another full-page cut (170 × 140 mm.) which is found on fol. cci b, is a close copy of the cut on the title of the *Esplandian* of 1525, printed in Rome, and also represents a mounted knight and attendants.   Throughout the text there are no less than 139 smaller cuts, the quality of which is of unequal merit.   There is no copy of this edition in the British Museum, and the writer's copy came from the Huth collection.

In 1536, Juan Cromberger produced an edition of the *De belo judayco* of Josephus, which, on account of the beauty of the title-page, is reproduced (Fig. 129).   It will be seen that the outside compartment border bears the initials S.M.D., and that the one at the foot of the page has the initials I.C. within a shield.   It has been suggested to me that these initials represent the initials of Jean Clein, a French woodcutter, but I can see nothing to support such a conclusion, and see no reason to doubt that the shield and initials form one of the numerous devices adopted by the Cromberger family.

In the next year (1537) an edition of the *Epistolas del glorioso doctor sant Hieronimo* appeared, which has a fine title-page within a decorative border.   Below the words of the title, which are printed in red, is a small and pleasing cut representing St. Jerome in the desert (Fig. 130).   On the verso of fol. viii of this book there is a very remarkable full-page cut on metal (265 × 187 mm.) showing St. Jerome and the lion, with a

Fhriftus factus est pro nobis obediés
vsqz ad morté: mortem aût crucis.

FIG. 127.—*Vita Christi Cartuxano*, Seville, Juan Cromberger, 1531.

FIG. 128.—*Amadis de gaula*, Seville, Juan Cromberger, 1535.
(Original printed in red and black.)

FIG. 129.—*Josepho de belo judayco*, Seville, Juan Cromberger, 1536.
(Reduced, original 247 × 167 mm., and printed in red and black.)

church, crucifix, and much other detail in the background (Fig.
131).   The cut is in criblée style and is from an original block
dating back to *c.* 1472, and was undoubtedly introduced into
Spain by some German printer.   This particular edition has
apparently escaped the notice of any bibliographer, and the copy
from which the reproductions have been made came from the
Royal Library of Carlos I., King of Portugal.

In 1541, the *Dialogo llamado Democrates* of Juan de Sepulveda
enables us to approximately fix the date of the death of Juan
Cromberger, as in the colophon we read, "en casa de Iuan
cröberjer difunto que dios aya."   Issued in quarto, the title of
the book is printed in red and black within an emblematic
woodcut border.   Below the colophon, there is a device of the
printer (Fig. 132), which, as far as is known, only appeared in
this book.   As will be seen, it consists of a circle with the
initials J.C. in the lower division and the Holy Lamb above,
surrounded by a glory.   At the sides are two ornamental columns,
with the spaces filled up with floral decoration.   There is no
copy of this book in the British Museum, and Escudero is only
able to cite, but with no particulars, a copy in an old index of
the Biblioteca del Noviciade de Madrid.

The year 1546 witnessed the production from the Cromberger press of one of the most entertaining picture books of the
period.   The work is an adaptation of the Fables of Bidpai,
written in Spanish and entitled *Libro Llamado Exemplario*, and is
expressed to have been printed "en las casas de Jacome Cromberger."   Haebler conjectures that "Jacome" may be Jacobo
returning to the scene of his former labours in order to take
charge of the press after the death of his son, Juan Cromberger.
Be this as it may, the book is a notable production, editions
of which had already appeared in 1534, 1537 and 1541, all
three having been printed by Juan Cromberger.   The 1541
edition, however, has the information in the colophon that Juan
Cromberger had died ("que santa gloria aya"), and it is clear

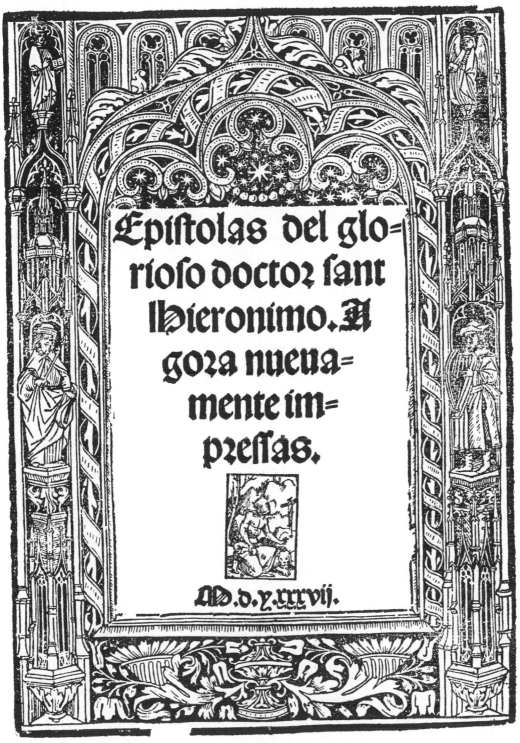

Epiſtolas del glo=
rioſo doctoz ſant
lḢieronimo.A
goza nueua=
mente im=
pzeſſas.

M.d.y.rrrvij.

FIG. 130.—S. Hieronymo—*Epistolas*, Seville, Juan Cromberger, 1537.
(Original printed in red and black.)

FIG. 131.—S. Hieronymo—*Epistolas*, Seville, Juan Cromberger, 1537.
(Reduced, original 265 × 187 mm.)

that this being the year of his death, that someone must have finished the publication, if not the printing, of the book.

The first edition actually printed in Spain was issued by the Hurus press in Zaragoza as early as 1493 (Haebler, 340), a book of the utmost rarity. The Seville edition of 1546, which we are now discussing, contains 122 cuts (averaging 56 × 74 mm.) and they are designed to illustrate the various fables and stories. Human beings, animals, and birds, are portrayed with much

FIG. 132.—Sepulveda—*Dialogo llamado Democrates*, Seville, Juan Cromberger, 1541.
(Device of printer.)

skill and rare humour (Figs. 133, 134, 135 and 136). The birds in particular are well drawn, and many of the cuts, consisting as they do of a few lines with a minimum of detail, or any undue elaboration in treatment, remind one of the work of Phil May in modern times, who was similarly happy in producing pleasing, skilful and artistic pictures, with a minimum of apparent effort, which is one of the characteristics of the artistic genius in any age.

A rare tract of Bartholome de las Casas, " the apostle of the Indians," being the one entitled, *Entre los remedios . . . para reformaciō de las Indias*, was printed "en la casa de Jacome Cromberger" as late as August, 1552. This first edition forms

FIG. 133.—*Libro Llamado Exemplario*, Seville, Jacome Cromberger, 1546.

one of nine tracts, printed in the same and the following year by Sebastian Trugillo, another Seville printer. The original editions of these tracts are of the utmost rarity, and eagerly sought for by

FIG. 134.—*Libro Llamado Exemplario*, Seville, Jacome Cromberger, 1546.

American collectors. It usually escapes attention that this particular one was a product of the Cromberger press. The tract, which is one of the longest in the series, consists of fifty-three printed leaves.   The title-page, here reproduced (Fig. 137), is from the volume of these nine tracts in the writer's collection.

FIG. 135.—*Libro Llamado Exemplario*, Seville, Jacome Cromberger, 1546.

It will be observed that already we begin to see some signs of the inferior work which characterised the second half of the century.

FIG. 136.—*Libro Llamado Exemplario*, Seville, Jacome Cromberger, 1546.

We have lingered upon the Cromberger press and its productions, covering as they did over half a century, because it is without doubt one which deservedly occupies a high place in

FIG. 137.—Bart. de Las Casas—*Entre los remedios . . . para reformacion de las Indias*, Seville, Jacome Cromberger, 1552. (Original printed in red and black.)

the typographical history not only of Spain, but of Europe, in this century.

FVE IMPRSSO EN SEVILLA.
en caſa de Martin de Monteſdoca.
Acaboſe a dos dias del mes
de Octubre de mill y
quinientos y cin-
cuenta y qua
tro años.

FIG. 138.—Fuenllana—*Libro de Musica*, Seville, M. de Montesdoca, 1554.
(Device of printer.)

We must content ourselves with brief references to the work of some of the other Seville printers.   In October, 1554, a *Libro de Musica* of Miquel de Fuenllana was produced " en casa de Martin de Montesdoca." The colophon and the striking device of the printer are here reproduced (Fig. 138). It will be seen that the cut is signed by the woodcutter with the initials

FIG. 139.—*Las ordenãcas de los Sastres* [Seville, M. de Montesdoca, 1554].
(Reduced, original printed on vellum, 241 × 170 mm.)

B.D.S. These initials lead me to attribute to this press an anonymously printed book of the same year, which is entitled, *Las ordenãcas de los Sastres y Calceteros y Jubeteros de esta ciudad de Sevilla.* From the reproduction of the title-page it will be seen (Fig. 139) that the book is a collection of the ordinances and decrees relating to the trades of tailors, stocking-makers and doublet-makers in this town.   The copy I possess, printed on vellum, is the only one I have been able to trace.   At the end, it bears the autograph certificate of Juan Cataño, a public notary and "Scrivano de su Magestad."   The decoration is good and

FIG. 140.—*Geometria y Traça para el oficio de los Sastres*, Seville, Fernando Diaz, 1588.

the initials B.D.S., presumably those of the woodcutter responsible for Montesdoca's device, appear at the foot of the Royal Arms which occupy most of the page.   While we are on the subject of tailors, mention may be made of a book, *Geometria y Traça para el oficio de los Sastres*, which was printed in Seville in 1588 by Fernandez Diaz.   The cut on the title, with its view of a contemporary tailor's shop, is of interest and is here reproduced (Fig. 140).

Juan Varela de Salamanca, another Seville printer, produced an edition of Petrarch's *De los remedios contra prospera y adversa fortuna* in 1524, the title-page of which is within some very

FIG. 141.—F. Petrarca—*Los Triumphos*, Seville, Juan Varela, 1532.

well-designed compartment borders.   His edition of the same author's *Triumphos* in 1532, has six large cuts which represent each of the triumphs.   From the reproduction of the " Triumpho de amor " (Fig. 141), it will be seen how crude the workmanship

FIG. 142.—Ambrosio Montesino—*Cancionero de diversas obras*, Seville, Dominico de Robertis, 1537.

is, compared with the Italian artist who illustrated the same book at Venice as early as 1491 with a series of cuts of exceptional beauty. Juan de Varela printed several romances of chivalry and similar books at Seville, and we shall come across him again when we deal with the early press at Granada. Dominico de Robertis, who also specialised in editions of these romances, had some pleasing decorative title-pages. I will take as an example his *Cancionero de diversas obras* of Ambrosio Montesino, a book of exceptional rarity, which he produced in 1537 (Fig. 142). The borders on this title are found in an equally rare and unrecorded edition of the *Refranes glosados*, which he printed in 1543. I am also inclined to attribute to him a *Cartilla para enseñar a leer*, which I found bound up at the end of the *Refranes glosados*, and which has a striking cut (138 × 108 mm.), showing a schoolmaster, birch in hand, surrounded by his pupils (Fig. 143), besides a series of smaller cuts throughout the text.

Fernando Diaz and Benito Lopez, who worked "en calle de la Sierpe," that most fascinating, extremely narrow and fashionable promenade, so beloved by the citizens of Seville, brought out in 1567 a *Repertorio de tiempos*, which is full of quaint illustrations. This book, which bears no definite trace of authorship, is probably an abridged edition of Jeronimo Chaves's translation of the astronomical encyclopedia of Sacro Bosco,[1] to which has been added a chronological account of notable incidents in Spanish history. It would seem to be the earliest book printed by Fernando Diaz, and I cannot trace Benito Lopez as a printer of any

[1] John of Holywood, otherwise known as Johannes de Sacro Bosco Anglicus, has always been reputed by bibliographers and others to come from Halifax in Yorkshire. Dr. J. F. Kellas Johnstone, in his *Bibliographia Aberdonensis* (now in the press), has exploded this hoary legend, and he shows that John of Holywood, in old Scots John Haliebus, was a native of a Dumfriesshire parish, and at one time a Trinity Friar at Aberdeen. In a copy of Conrad Gesner's *Bibliotheca Universalis*, Tiguri, 1545, in the Library of Aberdeen University, a contemporary scribe has written in the Index, after the name "De Sacrobusto, Joannes," the words "Haliewoode in Gallouidia Scotiae locus," and there would seem to be now very little doubt that he was in fact of Scots origin and birth.

FIG. 143.—*Cartilla para enseñar a leer* [Seville, Dominico de Robertis, *c.* 1543].

other book. After the title there is a cut (97 × 74 mm.) representing Astronomia enthroned, attended by Ptolemy and Urania, an obvious copy from the block used in the 1488 edition of Sacro Bosco's *Sphaera mundi*, printed at Venice by Hieron de Sanctis and Santritter. There is the usual cut of the "astronomical man" (167 × 99 mm.) and upwards of sixty other cuts representing the seasons, the months, the signs of the zodiac, eclipses of the moon, solar cycles, etc., etc. It was a very popular work at the time, and several editions were printed, not only by Diaz, but by J. Gutierrez. As is usual, however, the later editions are

FIG. 144.—S. Augustin—*Regla de vida Christiana*, Seville, Antonio Alvares, 1544.

characterised by progressive deterioration in the quality of the press-work and illustrations. Fernando Diaz will always be remembered as the printer of one of the most important works on heraldry published in Spain, the *Nobleza de Andaluzia* or Argote de Molina, printed in 1582, a book profusely illustrated with woodcut representations of the arms of the various noble families included in the work. In addition, Diaz was responsible for some of the illustrated medical works of Monardes, which dealt with the recent botanical and medical discoveries in the New World. Andres de Burgos, who had a press in Seville about 1542, produced several well-printed and decorated books.

His *Laberinto de amor* of Boccaccio in 1546, has a well-arranged decorative title-page and an alphabet of quaint and interesting initial letters.

Another printer who did good work in Seville, was Antonio Alvares, whose *Regla breve de vida Xp̄iana*, of 1544, is a nicely printed and decorated little book, of which I can trace no recorded copy.   It has small cuts of some merit (Fig. 144).   It would also seem to be the earliest book from this press.

We may leave Seville and its printing press in the sixteenth century, emphasising again that the family of Cromberger will always add lustre to the city and to the history of early printing in and out of the Peninsula.

¶ Regimiento contra la peste. Fecho por el insi
gne doctor Fernan baluarez: medico desus alte: as. Cathedratico de pri
ma en medicina eneíta vniuerfidad de Salamanca.

FIG. 145.—Alvarez.—*Regimiento contra la peste* [Salamanca, Juan Giesser, *c.* 1501].

CHAPTER XI.

SALAMANCA, BURGOS AND PAMPLONA.

AMONG the printers in Salamanca in the fifteenth century were Juan de Porras and Hans Giesser. Their work overlapped into the next century, and the *Regimiento contra la peste* of Alvarez, attributed to Giesser's press, *c.* 1501, or a little later, has an interesting cut on the title (Fig. 145).

Alphonsus de Porras and L. de Liondedeis, of whose press there are apparently only two recorded books, issued in 1524 the *Triumphus Christi Jesu contra infideles* of Christophorus de Sancto Antonio. This book has an elaborate title-page, printed in red and black, consisting of compartment cuts within decorative borders. The largest of these cuts, representing the Virgin and Child, is a little less conventional than is usual in its treatment (Fig. 146). Initial letters appear in this book, notably a fine capital T, with birds and foliage, white on a black ground, which are from the same blocks as used in the *Canonis Missae Expositio*, issued from the anonymous press, known as the " segundo grupo gótico," in this town in 1499 [1] (Haebler, 545). My copy of this book came from the library of the Marques de Astorga, and bears his early and extremely simple ex-libris (Fig. 147).

In 1530, there appeared in Salamanca an anonymously printed book, of which it would seem only one copy has survived. It is of English historical interest and its decorative title-page (Fig. 148) is not without some merit. It was written by

[1] For a reproduction of one of these initial letters, see Haebler, *The Early Printers in Spain and Portugal* (Plate XIII. (b)).

Alphonsus Virues, a Benedictine, and is one of the various controversial disquisitions relating to the divorce of Catherine of Aragon by Henry VIII.   I incline to think, from a comparison of types, that it may be attributed to the press of Juan de Junta,

FIG. 146.—C. de S. Antonio—*Triumphus Christi Jesu contra infideles*, Salamanca, A. de Porras y L. de Liondedeis, 1524.

one of the famous family of printers from Florence, who had established a press at Salamanca.   Among the productions from his press may be mentioned the following : The *Stabilimenta militum sacri ordinis divi Joannis hierosolymitani*, of July, 1534. This edition of the Statutes of the Order of St. John of Jerusalem is one of the earliest written in connexion with that world-famous body and is extremely rare. It has a fine woodcut title-page, printed in red and black, with the Arms of the Grand

BIBLIOTECA
DEL EXCMO.
SEÑOR MARQUES
DE ASTORGA.

FIG. 147.—Ex-libris of the Marques de Astorga.

FIG. 148.—Virues—*Tractatus de matrimonio Reg. Angliae,* Salamanca [Juan de Junta], 1530.

Master of the Order, and on the verso, those of the Grand Prior of Castile. There are large and well-executed woodcut capitals throughout the text, and at the end of the book a Bull of

Clement VII. in favour of the Order is printed, the first page of which is an interesting piece of decoration (Fig. 149).   The *Glosemata legum Tauri*, by Lopez de Palacios, Rubios, produced

FIG. 149.—*Stabilimenta militum sacri ordinis divi Joannis hierosolymitani*, Salamanca, Juan de Junta, 1534.
(Reduced, original 254 × 158 mm.)

in 1542, is specially notable for a fine series of decorative capitals (44 × 52 mm.), while the title-page, in red and black, is an effective piece of work.   In 1547, this printer was responsible for the *De justa haereticorum punitione* of Alphonsus de Castro, which has a good title-page with a portrait of the Emperor, Charles V., in the top compartment. It is of interest to recall that this was the work which the Emperor's Confessor, Pedro de Soto, handed to Francisco de Enzinas, the first translator of

FIG. 150.—Ciruelo—*Reprovacion de las supersticiones*, Salamanca, P. Tobans, 1540.
Also,
Lareda—*Subida del monte Sion*, Medina del Campo, Pedro de Castro, 1542.

the New Testament into Spanish, when he was imprisoned as a result of his attempt to introduce the New Testament in the vulgar tongue to his fellow-countrymen.

The *Obras de Xenophon*, of 1552, is also a good example of

the work of this printer. The large cut of the Royal Arms, printed in red and black, which adorns the title, is specially well-designed and executed.

Pierres Tobans, who printed in 1540 an edition of Pedro

FIG. 151.—Luys de Granada—*Memorial de la vida Christiana*, Salamanca, D. de Portonariis, 1569.

de Ciruelo's *Reprovacion de las supersticiones y Hechizerias*, besides printing at this town, worked also at Medina del Campo and Zamora. In this book we find the title surrounded by an architectural and emblematic border, the top compartment of which is signed I.D.V. (Juan de Vingles), while on the verso, there is a crucifixion cut with the monogram of Vingles (Fig. 150). Both this title border and the cut are to be found later in Lareda's *Subida del monte Sion*, printed by Pedro de Castro at Medina del Campo in 1542. There are also decorative capitals

FIG. 152.—*Pasionario*, Salamanca, M. Gast, 1570.

common to both books. Domingo de Portonariis, who held the post of " Impressor de su Catholica Magestad," printed in 1569 an edition of the famous *Memorial de la vida Christiana* of Luys de Granada, which has some cuts not without interest. We reproduce one which represents St. Peter being rescued from the waves (Fig. 151).

Matias Gast was a prolific printer at Salamanca between 1562 and 1599. Attention may be called to two of his books in 1570. The first is a *Pasionario*, or liturgical choir book,

FIG. 153.—*Pasionario*, Salamanca, M. Gast, 1570.

prepared by Juan de Palencia, a Dominican, and is a beautifully printed piece of work, remarkable for its wealth of well-designed and extremely decorative initial letters, which are printed in red and black, as well as for a good cut of St. Dominic on the title (124 × 95 mm.), which is another of the few examples of signed work by the Spanish woodcutters (Fig. 152). The character of the woodcut capitals will be seen from the capital P, taken from the recto of the first leaf of the text[1] (Fig. 153). The music in the book is on a five-line red stave, with square black notes. This edition has apparently escaped the attention of bibliographers.

The second of the books printed in this year is a *Dioscorides*, translated by Andres de Laguna. It is a substantial folio volume, full of quaint cuts, which depict animals, birds, medicinal plants and various country scenes. The illustration of the farmer and

FIG. 154.—Dioscorides—*Acerca de la materia medicinal*, Salamanca, Mathias Gast, 1570.

his wife engaged in shearing their sheep will show the crude character of these cuts (Fig. 154).

The *Sphaera mundi* of Francisco Sanchez, which Guillermo Foquel printed in 1588, is an interesting little octavo volume, in which are found numerous cuts illustrating the Heavens, the signs of the Zodiac and other astronomical diagrams.

Miguel Serrano de Vargas printed in 1589 *El Triumpho de Nuestro Señor* of Luys de Tobar. It contains sixty-seven woodcuts

---

[1] This capital letter is either taken from the same block, or a very faithful copy of one which appeared in a *Graduale*, printed at Turin in 1514 by Petrus Paulus and Galeazius de Porris.

(some repeated) which illustrate scenes in the life of Christ. I have not been able to trace the history of these cuts which are obviously very much earlier than the book, and in all probability of the late fifteenth century (Fig. 155).

FIG. 155.—Luys de Tobar—*El Triumpho de Nuestro Señor*, Salamanca, Miguel Serrano de Vargas, 1589.

BURGOS.

Fadrique de Basilea and Juan de Burgos, the two printers in this town in the fifteenth century, both continued to print in the early part of the succeeding one.   We have already directed attention to some of their work (pp. 76-88).   Andres de Burgos, whose press at Granada we shall have occasion to mention later, printed at Burgos in the early years of the sixteenth century. His edition of *Las Decadas de tito livio*, printed in 1505, has on the title-page a cut which as we have already mentioned (p. 87) was used by Juan de Burgos in 1497.   It is now found surrounded by two side borders, and on the verso there is a full-page crucifixion cut, and on the first leaf of the text a beautiful woodcut capital, white on a red background, attracts attention. Following the colophon is the device of Andres de Burgos, which as far as I know, only appears in this book (Fig. 156).

FIG. 156.—Livy—*Las Decadas*, Burgos, Andres de Burgos, 1505.
(Device of printer.)

Alonso de Melgar, who printed from 1519 until after the middle of the century, produced well-printed and decorative books. His *Arte de cõfessiõ breve*, which he printed in December 1519, has an attractive and simple title-page, at the foot of which there is a small and graceful cut representing two angels

(Fig. 157). The book is unrecorded, and my copy was one of the books in the Royal Library of Carlos I., King of Portugal.

Juan de Junta, whose work at Salamanca we have already noticed, had a press at Burgos for over thirty years. He printed a number of Statutes and similar legal works in his early years.

FIG. 157.—*Arte de cõfessiõ breve*, Burgos, Alonso de Melgar, 1519.

A good example of this period is afforded by an *Aranzel,* or *Quaderno de las ordenancas hechas por sus altezas cerca de la ordẽ judicial* (Fig. 158). It will be observed that in the lower border of the title the first two figures of the century, "15," are inserted, the remaining two being left blank for insertion as occasion might require. In this example, which is elsewhere dated 1538, they have been omitted. In 1550 he printed the *Norte de los estados*, of Francisco de Ossuna, the title-page of which is here reproduced (Fig. 159).

As an example of the manner in which the romances of

FIG. 158.—*Aranzel*, Burgos, Juan de Junta, 1538.
(Reduced, original 247 × 155 mm.)

chivalry were produced at this period, we reproduce the title-page of an edition in 1554 of *La historia de los dos nobles cavalleros Oliveros de Castilla y Artus de Algarve* (Fig. 160). The book, quarto in size, has some good initial letters, but with the exception of the cut on the title, is otherwise not illustrated.

This is one of the very early romances of chivalry, and was first printed in Burgos by Fadrique de Basilea in 1499 (Haebler,

1 5 5 0

Norte de los estados:
En que se da regla de biuir a los Mācebos: y a los Casados: y a los Biudos: y a todos los Cōtinentes. Y se tratā muy por estenso los remedios del desastrado Casamiēto: enseñando q̄ tal ha de ser la vida del christiano casado. Compuesto por el reuerendo padre fray frācisco de Ossuna: cōmissario general de la ordē de sant francisco. En las prouincias de las Indias del mar occeano.

FIG. 159.—Francisco de Ossuna—*Norte de los estados*, Burgos, Juan de Junta, 1550. (Reduced, original 180 × 125 mm., printed in red and black.)

494). It deals with the Kings of England and Ireland and some of the scenes are laid in London. This particular edition

FIG. 160.—*La historia de los dos nobles cavalleros Oliveros de Castilla y Artus de Algarve*, Burgos, Juan de Junta, 1554.

of 1554 is unrecorded, and the copy in my possession is the only one I have been able to trace. The popularity of these romances is shown by the fact that in the same year another edition of this particular one was printed in Burgos by Pedro de Santillana. A copy of it was sold in the Britwell Court Sale of 1920, fetching £50, and is now in the British Museum. *Los Dichos, o sentencias de los siete Sabios de Grecia, en metro*, by Hernan Lopez

FIG. 161.—Lopez de Yanguas—*Los Dichos de los siete Sabios de Grecia*, Burgos, *c*. 1600.
(Reduced, original 173 × 114 mm.)

de Yanguas, which appeared about this time, or a little later, "en la Imprenta de Burgos," affords an illustration of the crude chapbook of the time of which very few have survived (Fig. 161). The *Tractado de las Drogas, y medicinas de las Indias* of Christobal Acosta, which was issued from the press of Martin de Victoria in 1578, is full of woodcuts showing the plants and medicinal herbs to be found in the New World. The book has also some good initial letters.

The last of the Burgos books which we will mention is an edition of the *Chronica del Famoso Cavallero Cid Ruy Diez Campeador*, which was issued "en la Imprimeria de Phillipe de Iunta y Iuan Baptista Varesio" in 1593.   The title, printed in

Cid Ruydiez Campeador.

Fig. 162.—*Chronica del Famoso Cavallero Cid Ruy Diez Compeador*, Burgos, P. de Junta y Juan B. Varesio, 1593.
(Reduced, original 234 × 151 mm.)

red and black, has a large cut of the Royal Arms, and on fol. 278 there is a full-page cut representing the Cid on horseback, surmounted by his Arms.   This cut is from the same block as used in the rare first edition of this chronicle, which Fadrique de Basilea printed in 1512 (Fig. 162).

PAMPLONA.

In the fifteenth and sixteenth centuries Pamplona was a town of some importance, and therefore it is somewhat surprising to find that the art of printing was in the hands of an extremely limited number of printers. We have seen that Arnaldo Guillen de Brocar was the only printer of incunabula, while Thomas Porralis and Mathias Mares were the two printers of any importance who exercised their calling there in the sixteenth century. We will take as an example of the work of Porralis two books, one his *Historia del Duque Carlos de Borgoña*, by Pedro de Aguilon, which he printed in 1586. This book has a crude full-page portrait of "Charles the Bold" on the recto of the last leaf, and is expressed to be "antes muerto que rendido." The other book is his edition of the *Cronica del Serenissimo Rey Don Iuan II.*, by Perez de Guzman, which Porralis published in 1590 and 1591, taking as his text the famous first edition which had been printed at Logroño in 1517.

The book has a good decorative woodcut title-page, printed in red and black, besides some initial letters of good workmanship. There seem to have been two issues of this edition, as I have copies dated respectively 1590 and 1591.

One of the first, if not actually the first book which Mathias Mares printed at Pamplona was the *Viaje de la Tierra Santa y Descripcion de Ierusalen*, of Iuan Ceverio de Vera, in which some poor cuts of the Holy Symbols illustrate the poverty of the book decoration of the period. In other respects, the book is of some interest, as the author (who died in 1600) spent forty years of his life in America, before he made his visit to the Holy Land. In his Prologue, he refers to Columbus and the discovery of the New World, and discusses in another chapter the commercial relations of Italy, England and France with America, while there are also interesting references to the Canary Islands, Quito and Peru.

Pamplona may be said to have added very little to the history of our subject.

CHAPTER XII.

VALLADOLID AND TOLEDO.

REFERENCE has already been made to the first recorded piece of printing at Valladolid, which came from the press of Nuestra Señora del Prado, and was a *Bula de S. Salvador de Avila* (see p. 7), in 1481.

The first sixteenth-century printer was Diego de Gumiel, and perhaps the most interesting specimen of his work is to be found in the *Mar de istorias*, by Hernan Perez de Guzman, which he printed in 1512. One of the great historical classics of Spanish literature in the fifteenth century, the last part of the book contains the author's original memoirs of his own times. The title-page is a fine and severe example of xylographic printing, and the first page of the text is surrounded by an elaborate border of Arabesques. The beautiful device of Gumiel is found here surrounded by four small compartment cuts of Saints, all within borders, the whole effect adding a pleasing finish to the decoration of the book. This seems to have been the last book which Gumiel printed before he went to Valencia, and none of his earlier work at Valladolid calls for any special notice.

Arnaldo Guillen de Brocar, whose press at Alcalá was one of the most famous in the sixteenth century, produced various books at Valladolid between the years 1514 and 1519. An un-recorded edition of *Las Meditaciones* of St. Augustin, printed by him in 1515, has a pleasing cut of the Saint on the title, which is repeated in the *Soliloquios del anima a dios*, which forms the second part of the book [1] (Fig. 163). A specially good woodcut

---

[1] Cf. the cut on the title of the *Cancionero de diversas obras* of Montesino, printed at Seville in 1537 (Fig. 142), which is a copy in reverse.

capital, white on a black background (fol. 70b), depicts Joseph, Mary and the Infant Christ.

Nicolas Tierri, who printed here from 1525 until about 1539, had the distinction of printing the first edition of the *Relox de principes*, the famous work of Antonio de Guevara,

FIG. 163.—S. Augustin—*Las Meditaciones*, Valladolid, A. G. de Brocar, 1515.

Bishop of Mondoñedo, and the official Chronicler to the Emperor, Charles V. This book was translated into various European languages, and is familiar to English readers in the translation of Sir Thomas North, an edition of which was reissued as recently as 1919. To return to the first Spanish edition produced by Tierri in 1529. The general title is a fine piece of decorative work, in red and black, the compartment borders, architectural and emblematic in character, being well arranged and admirably designed. Each of the three books in the volume has a separate

FIG. 164.—Antonio de Guevara—*Relox de principes*, Valladolid, Nicolas Tierri, 1529.
(Reduced, original 251 × 177 mm., printed in red and black.)

title, and the first of these is here reproduced (Fig. 164). It affords a good example of the work of this printer, and the initials of the woodcutter, A.O.M., appear in the top compartment.

Diego Fernandez de Cordova was at work in this town in

1538, in which year he printed a *Breviarū monasticum*. The title-page here reproduced from the only known copy on vellum (Fig. 165), has an unusual cut representing two hands holding

Sunt gemini fratres virides qui munere palmas.
Sanguinei gestant pręmia martyrii.

Breuiariū monasticum
secundum consuetudinem ordinis sancti Benedi
cti de obseruantia congregationis Coeno=
bii sancti Benedicti Uallisoletani.

Ex decreto capituli generalis.
Anni. M. D. xxxviii.

Excusum apud insigne sanctorum mar=
tyrum Facundi ꞇ Primitiui Coeno
bium. Didacus Fernandez de
Cordoua excudebat.

FIG. 165.—*Breviarum Benedictinum*, Valladolid, D. Fernandez de Cordova, 1538.
(Reduced, original 177 × 115 mm., printed on vellum in red and black.)

palm leaves. In the next year (1539), an anonymously printed book, *Las Cient nouellas de micer Juan Bocacio Florentino*, an extremely rare edition of the Decameron, may safely be attributed to this printer. The beautiful woodcut title-page, with nine

FIG. 166.—*Las Cient nouellas de micer Juan Bocacio*, Valladolid [Diego Fernandez de Cordova], 1539.
(Reduced, original 260 × 164 mm.)

compartments, contains figures and scenes illustrating the text, and upper and lower borders of grotesque cupids (Fig. 166).

Francisco Fernandez de Cordova, who was probably a son of Diego, held the position of King's Printer, and his press lasted for the long period of upwards of thirty years. In 1545, he printed the *Arte de navegar* of Pedro de Medina, the first practical treatise on the science of navigation. It was an extremely popular work, making, as it did, a strong appeal to those who, with profound interest and attention, were following the exploits of Columbus and his successors. It subsequently was translated into various European languages, the English edition appearing in 1581 and being speedily thumbed out of existence. The only known copy of this English edition which survives in either the United Kingdom or America, appeared in the London Sale Rooms in 1922, and although not very adequately catalogued, fetched the not inconsiderable price of £260.

The first Spanish edition, which we are now discussing, is scarcely less rare. Salvá only knew of some six copies, and in referring to his own copy, now in the writer's collection, remarks with pride, "el mio es bello." The book is fully illustrated, and as will be seen from the reproduction of the title-page (Fig. 167), which is printed in red and black, it is a typical example of the decoration of the period. Of the cuts in the book, the one that appears on the title of "Libro segundo" is a remarkable and striking one (Fig. 168). Medina, who informs us in this book that at one time he had followed the sea as his profession, was afterwards appointed as an Examiner of the Pilots for the Indies and acquired a great reputation as a cosmographer. This first edition contains on the recto of fol. xxii. an extremely rare map of the "Nuevo mundo" (Fig. 169). The map represents a flat surface, extending from 65 degrees North to 18 degrees South latitude, and from the West Coast of Mexico to the Gulf of Guinea in longitude. Florida and Peru are indicated, and in the Old World, England, Scotland and Ireland find their appropriate, if, as far as type is concerned, somewhat diminutive place.

FIG. 167.—Pedro Medina—*Arte de navegar*, Valladolid, F. Fernandez de Cordova,
1545.
(Reduced, original 264 × 166 mm., printed in red and black.)

FIG. 168.—Pedro Medina—*Arte de navegar*, Valladolid, F. Fernandez de Cordova, 1545.

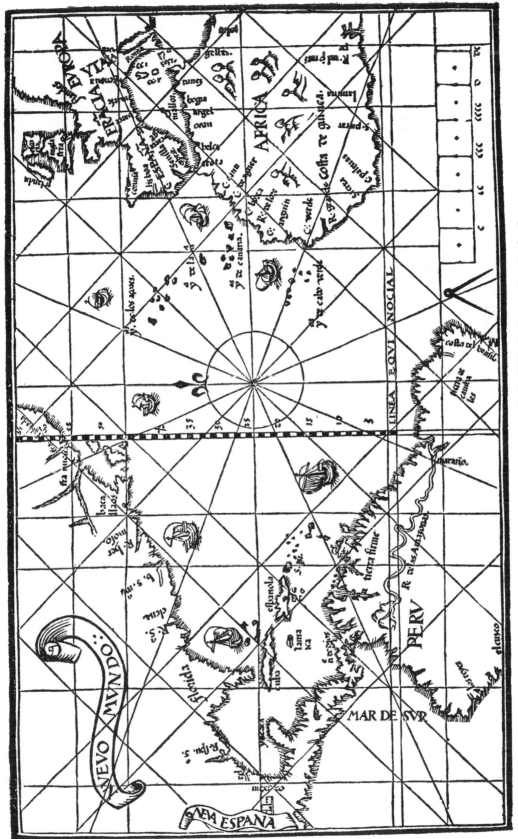

FIG. 169.—Pedro Medina—*Arte de navegar*, Valladolid, F. Fernandez de Cordova, 1545.

There are several other illustrations in the book, notably a fine piece of red colour printing, forming the title to the fourth book in the volume, in which the Sun is given the form of a somewhat stern and forbidding human face. The book as a whole is a very interesting and important example of the illustration and decoration of an early Spanish scientific treatise.

As an illustration of the catholicity of the subjects to which this printer devoted his press, we may mention the *Provechoso tratado de cambios y contrataciones de mercaderes, y reprovacion de usura* of Christoval de Villalon. It is a well-decorated and printed book on the prosaic subject of usury, with chapters on

FIG. 170.—Villalon—*Provechoso tratado de cambios,* Valladolid, F. Fernandez de Cordova, 1546.

Rates of Exchange, Brokers, Bankers, Interest and Rents. It is one of the first books to bear on the title any formal admission of the censorship of books by the Holy Office ; the words being : " Visto y examinado por los señores del muy alto Consejo, y sancta Inquisicion, Año de 1546." A specimen of a fine alphabet of woodcut capitals is here reproduced (Fig. 170). The same printer published in two volumes, in 1550 and 1552, *Las quatrocientas repuestas* of Luis de Escobar. The author was a bedridden Franciscan friar of literary tastes, to whom the Almirante de Castilla and his friends addressed some 400 questions and riddles, which Escobar re-wrote with their answers in verse. Both volumes have fine woodcut title-pages and the initial capital letters are good, while the device of the printer (Fig. 171), which appears in the second volume, is not without interest. Another notable book from this press was an edition in 1552 of *Las coplas, con glosa de moral sentido en prosa*, of Iorge Manrique, which has a well-designed decorative title-page, printed in red and black, containing the woodcut Arms of Juan Vasquez de Molina, "secretario de su Magestad." This work of Manrique

FIG. 171.—Escobar—*Las quatrocientas repuestas*, Valladolid, F. Fernandez de Cordova, 1552.
(Device of the printer.)

has been immortalised by Longfellow, some lines of whose translation, of singular beauty, one may be permitted to quote :—

> Our lives are rivers, gliding free
> To that unfathomed, boundless sea,
>   The silent grave !
> Thither all earthly pomp and boast
> Roll, to be swallowed up and lost
>   In one dark wave.
>
> Thither the mighty torrents stray,
> Thither the brook pursues its way,
>   And tinkling rill.
> There all are equal.   Side by side,
> The poor man and the son of pride
>   Lie calm and still.

The only other printer at this town whose work requires attention, is Sebastian Martinez, whose *Chronica del Rey Don Alonso el Sabio*, produced in 1554, is a good specimen of decorative printing. The title, printed in red and black, has a portrait of Alonso, the borders being bold and well designed. The life of Alonso's son, "Sancho el Bravo," is also in this work, and its separate title-page has a cut which would seem to be older than the book. The initials of the printer (possibly he was also the woodcutter) appear in the lower compartment border. There is also a pleasing set of woodcut capitals. If Valladolid was not remarkable for any special development in the art of book decoration and illustration, it can at least lay claim to have produced some well-printed and decorated works of no small interest in the literary history of Spain in the sixteenth century.

TOLEDO.

We have already dealt with the sixteenth-century work of Pedro Hagembach, when considering his incunabula (see p. 90), and the next printer in chronological order, is Iuan Varela de Salamanca, who had a press in the town between 1510 and 1514. His *Espejo de la conciencia*, of 1513, has a cut on the title representing St. Francis praying before a crucifix, but with this, and similar trifling exceptions, his work in Toledo, as regards the decoration and illustration of his books, was negligible.

Juan de Villaquiran, whose press lasted for over a quarter of a century, was a prolific printer, but his illustrated productions were not very numerous. He printed an edition of Livy's *Las Decadas* in 1516, in which there is a cut on the title-page in which the author is shown writing his book at a table, a conventional treatment of a title-page which was very common among the early printers of Spain. Again, in 1520, we find his *Valerio de las historias scholasticas*, of Diego de Almela, has its title-page decorated with a cut, in which a king is shown seated on his throne and surrounded by attendants, which also shows

FIG. 172.—Ambrosio Montesino—*Epistolas i evangelios*, Toledo, Juan de Villaquiran y Juan de Ayala, 1535.

little or no originality in design. However, he was capable of producing a well-illustrated book, and his magnum opus in this direction was his edition of the *Epistolas i evangelios por todo el año* by Ambrosio Montesino. The edition which we will now describe he printed in conjunction with Juan de Ayala in 1535. Pérez Pastor indicates that there were editions printed by Villaquiran alone in 1512 and 1532, but had not seen a copy of either

FIG. 173.—Ambrosio Montesino—*Epistolas i evangelios*, Toledo, Juan de Villaquiran y Juan de Ayala, 1535.

of them and gives no particulars. He cites the 1512 edition on the authority of a catalogue of the books in the University Library of Valencia, and the 1532 edition from the Abecedarium Bibliothecæ Columbinæ. To revert to the edition of 1535. It is a folio volume, with the title in red and black, within a woodcut ornamental border, the top and lower compartments of which are signed with the initials I.D.V. (Iuan de Vingles). The first initial letter E in the title is in the form of a dragon, being printed in red and black in the manner of chiaroscuro. On the verso of fol. 6, facing the first leaf of the text, there is a magnificent crucifixion cut, within borders (Fig. 172). It will be observed that the initials D.N. are prominent in the background. Whether these refer to our Lord, or are the initials of the woodcutter, must remain a matter of conjecture. The cut is certainly of unusual merit, the numerous figures and horses in the foreground being very well executed. The side borders, within which the cut is enclosed, consisting of angels, are also to be

FIG. 174.—Ambrosio Montesino—*Epistolas i evangelios*, Toledo, Juan de Villaquiran y Juan de Ayala, 1535.

noted. The first page of the text is a striking piece of work within a woodcut border, the inner compartment of which has an interesting little cut at the top, while a large capital and a cut in the text add distinction to the page. The book, which consists of six preliminary and 230 leaves of text, is profusely illustrated with a series of upwards of 250 small cuts, depicting incidents in the life of Christ. They are quaint in design and obviously far older than the date of this book and in all probability of fifteenth-century workmanship. Two specimens of these cuts are here reproduced (Figs. 173 and 174).

Toledo was one of the towns to which Arnaldo Guillen de Brocar made flitting visits with his press, and during the three years between 1519 and 1521, we find his Toledo imprint. The *Compendium totius sacre scripture* of 1519, and his *Sedulii paschale cū cōmento Antonii Nebrisseñ*, printed in 1520, both bear the striking form of device which he used in his Toledo books (Fig. 175). It is the same device as he used at Alcalá in the Complutensian Polyglot Bible, but has a different motto within the triangular shield. Brocar only printed some five books at Toledo and they are all of some rarity.

Ramon de Petras, another printer at this town who was at work at the time, was responsible for two important books from the literary point of view, the *Libro de cozina* of Ruberto de Nola, in 1525, the first Spanish cookery book,[1] and an early edition of the *Cancionero general* of Hernando del Castillo, both of which books are exceptionally rare. The woodcut title-page of the *Libro de cozina* is a careful piece of work (Fig. 176), while the full-page cut on the last leaf is not without interest (Fig. 177). The title-page of the *Cancionero general* is well printed in red and black within a fine border of architectural design. The device of this printer is reproduced (Fig. 178).

Gasper de Avila, whose press only lasted five years (1525-1529), has one illustrated book to his credit of outstanding interest and importance. Bartholomew Anglicus, sometimes, and inaccurately, called Bartholomew de Glanville, was the author of the famous encyclopedia of the Middle Ages, known as *De proprietatibus rerum*. It was first printed at Cologne c. 1472, and some of the press work in connexion with the edition is attributed to Caxton, if we are to accept literally the verses at the end of Wynkyn de Worde's first English edition which appeared in 1495. They read as follows :—

---

[1] The *Doctrina del Art de coch* by Nola had appeared in Catalán in Barcelona in 1520, the title-page of which has an interesting cut in red and black, showing the interior of a kitchen, with a cook at work with his assistants and various culinary implements.

"And also of your charyte call to remembraunce
    The soule of William Caxton, the fyrst prynter of this boke
In laten tongue at Coleyn, himself to avaunce
    That every well disposyd man may thereon loke."

FIG. 175.—Nebrissensis—*Sedulii paschale*, Toledo, A. G. de Brocar, 1520.

⸿Libro de cozina cõpuesto por

maestre Ruberto de Mola cozinero ꝗ̃ fue õl seremíssimo señor rey dõ Fer
nãdo de Napoles: de muchos potajes y salsas y guisados paral tnépo õl
carnal y dela ꝗ̃resma: y mãjares y salsas y caldos para doliétes de muy
grã sustãcia. y frutas de sarten: y marçapanes: y otras cosas muy puccho
sas. y del sernicio y offici os delas casas delos reyes y grãdes señores y ca
ualleros: cada vno como a de seruir su cargo. y el trinchãte como a de cor
tar todas maneras de carnes. y de aues. y otras muchas cosas enel aña=
didas muy prouechosas. Muy bien corregido y emendado.

⸿Cõ preuilegio real de diez años

que niguno lo pueda imprimir en todos los reynos y señorios delas ma
gestades: so las penas contenidas enel dicho preuilegio.

Fig. 176.—Nola—*Libro de cozina*, Toledo, Ramon de Petras, 1525.

The first edition of the book in Spanish was printed in Toulouse by Henrique Meyer in 1494, with some fine cuts. The edition of Gasper de Avila, which we are now discussing, was the first actually printed in Spain, and the cuts are entirely different. The title-page is printed in red and black, and above the intitulation are nine compartment cuts. The principal one of these is printed in red and shows the Almighty engaged in

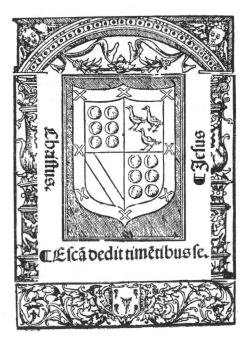

FIG. 177.—Nola—*Libro de cozina*, Toledo, Ramon de Petras, 1525.
(Reduced, original 165 × 118 mm.)

creating the world, while the other cuts represent the various stages of the creation. Among the cuts are representations of the Anatomical Man, a patient in bed suffering from headache ("dolor de cabeça") (Fig. 179), and other illustrations devoted to astronomical subjects, country scenes (Figs. 180 and 181), and natural history.

Miguel de Eguia, a famous Alcalá printer, seems to have had a press at Toledo from which he issued at intervals a few books.   Dr. Burger registers four of these, all of them printed in 1526 and 1527 and none of them of any importance from our

FIG. 178.—*Cancionero general*, Toledo, Ramon de Petras, 1527.
(Device of printer.)

point of view.   I am able, however, to give an excellent example of the illustrated work of Eguia at Toledo, in the shape of an

FIG. 179.—Bartholomaeus Anglicus—*De proprietatibus rerum en romance*, Toledo,
Gaspar de Avila, 1529.

unrecorded edition of *La vida de la sacratissima virgē maria señora nuestra* of Miguel Perez, which appeared in 1526, and would

FIG. 180.—Bartholomaeus Anglicus—*De proprietatibus rerum en romance*, Toledo, Gaspar de Avila, 1529.

FIG. 181.—Bartholomaeus Anglicus—*De proprietatibus rerum en romance*, Toledo, Gaspar de Avila, 1529.

seem to be the first edition in Castilian. The book was first
printed in the Limosin dialect at Valencia by Nicolas Spindeler

FIG. 182.—M. Perez—*La vida de la sacratissima virgẽ*, Toledo, Miguel de Eguia,
1526.

in 1494 (Haebler, 540), and apparently did not contain any cuts.
This edition of Eguia in 1526 is, however, well illustrated with

FIG. 183.—M. Perez—*La vida de la sacratissima virgẽ*, Toledo, Miguel de Eguia,
1526.

small cuts representing scenes in the lives of our Lord and of the
Virgin Mary. Two specimens are here reproduced (Figs. 182
and 183) from a copy which came from the Royal Library of

FIG. 184.—-Balt. Castiglione—*Los Quatro Libros del Cortesano*, Toledo [Juan de Ayala], 1539.

Carlos I., King of Portugal. It is a well-printed small quarto volume, and in addition to the cuts has some excellent woodcut capitals. The colophon reads : " A loor y gloria de nuestro señor Jesu Christo y de la/sacratissima virgē sancta maria su madre fue/impressa la presente obra llamada la vida/de nuestra señora en la muy noble y im/perial cibdad de Toledo ; en casa de/Miguel de Eguia. A veynte y/nueve dias de nouiembre./ Año de mill y quinien/tos y veynte y/seys años./ "

The name of the next printer, Juan de Ayala, introduces us to one, who by himself and his successors carried on a press in Toledo from 1530 and onwards for nearly half a century. At the commencement of his operations in the town, he worked in conjunction with Juan de Villaquiran (see p. 220). In 1539, however, we find him working alone and producing an edition of *Los Quatro Libros del Cortesano*, of Baltasar Castellon (Balt. Castiglione). The title-page of this book, with its woodcut border, is here reproduced (Fig. 184) from the Salvá copy. This is the earliest edition of this well-known work in Spanish, of which only a few copies seem to have survived, there being no trace now of editions alleged to have been printed at Barcelona in 1534 and 1535.

In 1542 Ayala printed the *Samarites Comedia de Samaritano Evangelico* of Petrus Papeus, from the title-page of which is reproduced the woodcut Arms of Fernando de Lunar (Fig. 185). This is one of the earliest comedies printed in Spain, and is edited with notes by Alejo Vanegas (or Venegas), who has been the subject of an enthusiastic eulogy by Gregorio Mayans in his " Specimen Bibliothecae hispano-ma jansianae." Copies of this comedy are seemingly very rare, and I am only able to trace one in the provincial Library of Toledo, in addition to the one in my own collection. In 1546 he printed a *Tractado de los prestamos que passan entre mercaderes y tractantes*, a curious treatise on mercantile laws and customs, which has a cut on the title-page representing a Monk with St. Francis, both of them engaged in capturing a serpent, which is apparently coming out of a money bag, which is no doubt designed to illustrate the ethical reflections upon the commercial morals and methods of the period, which form a large portion of the book.

As a specimen of the late work of this printer, mention

FIG. 185.—P. Papeus—*Samarites Comedia de Samaritano Evangelico*, Toledo, Juan de Ayala, 1542.

may be made of an edition of the *Vitas Patrum* of St. Jerome, which he printed in 1553. The title-page of this folio volume is printed in red and black within fine decorative borders which bear the initials I.D.V. (Juan de Vingles) and enclose a pleasing cut of St. Jerome, which is reproduced (Fig. 186). This particular work of St. Jerome seems to be particularly scarce in this

Spanish translation. There are two fifteenth century editions, one attributed to Pablo Hurus at Zaragoza, *c.* 1491, and the other to the "Segundo grupo gótico" at Salamanca in October, 1498. Of these, there are only single copies of each surviving (Haebler, 335(5) and 336), and apparently the same fate has fallen upon this edition of 1553, as I am unable to find any trace of any other copy than the one in my possession, which was

FIG. 186.—S. Hieronymo—*Vitas Patrum*, Toledo, Juan de Ayala, 1553.

formerly in the Royal Library of Carlos I., King of Portugal. There is no other recorded edition in the sixteenth century.

The only other book from the Ayala press which need detain us is *La Segunda Parte de la Fabrica del Universo* of Bernaldo Perez de Vargas, a folio volume, which, according to the colophon, he printed in 1560, although 1563 appears on the title-page, which has a large cut of three lilies on a shield, surmounted by a crown. On the second leaf, there is a pleasing cut of Arms, and throughout the volume numerous cuts and

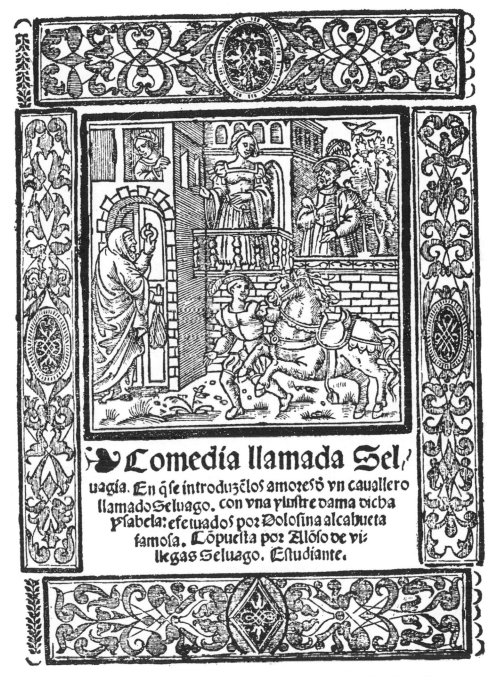

FIG. 187.—Alonso de Villegas—*Comedia llamada Selvagia*, Toledo, Juan Ferrer, 1554.
(Original printed in red and black.)

diagrams, including a good example of the "Anatomical Man." The book ends with "un breve summario de cosas notables acontecidas en el mundo," which has a separate woodcut title. When this book was printed, Ayala had died, because we read in the colophon, "que sancta gloria aya." The first part of this work was never printed and only exists in a MS.

Juan Ferrer, another of the printers who worked here in

FIG. 188.—F. Hernandez Blasco—*Universal Redempcion*, Toledo, viuda de Juan de la Plaza, 1589.

the second half of the century, was responsible for printing the *Comedia llamada Selvagia* of Alonso de Villegas, one of the rarest comedies of the Spanish theatre. The cut on the title-page (Fig. 187) gives a view of a stage, with a scene from the comedy, and is an early representation of a Spanish theatre.

In 1589, there appeared a second edition of the *Universal Redempcion*, a poem by Francisco Hernandez Blasco. This was printed by the widow of Juan de la Plaza. It is illustrated with fifty-six curious cuts, some of which are repeated, and all of which bear obvious signs of Italian inspiration. In a preliminary note we are told that the author himself was responsible for these cuts, and each of them bears the initials F.H. Two of them are reproduced (Figs. 188 and 189), and it will be seen that the one in which two angels appear bears the date 1587.

FIG. 189.—F. Hernandez Blasco—*Universal Redempcion*, Toledo, viuda de Juan de la Plaza, 1589.

Toledo, like Valladolid, was not remarkable for any very special development in book decoration or illustration, but her printers maintained a good average of workmanship and artistic design, and certainly the deterioration at the end of the century was not so marked here as in some other towns of equal importance.

DIALOGOS
DE MEDALLAS
INSCRICIONES
y otras antiguedades.

Ex bibliotheca Ant. Augustini
Archiepiscopi Tarraconen.

Con licencia del Superior

En Tarragona por Felipe Mey.

1587.

Hadriani Beverlandi

Oxoniae.

1691.

FIG. 190.—Antonio Augustin—*Dialogos de medallas*, Tarragona, Felipe Mey, 1587.

CHAPTER XIII.

TARRAGONA, ZAMORA AND TORTOSA.

TARRAGONA.

JUAN ROSEMBACH in the fifteenth century overshadowed all his successors in this town, and we find that Felipe Mey and Felipe Roberto were the only two sixteenth-century printers of any importance. Mey's chief title to fame was his edition of the *Dialogos de medallas inscriciones y otras antiguedades* of Antonio Augustin, Archbishop of Tarragona. This first edition of 1587 is of such rarity that Sr. Don Angel del Arco, the bibliographer of this town,[1] among his reproductions of title-pages, gives one of this book, which he rightly describes as "Portada apócrifa," as will be at once seen from a comparison with the one here reproduced (Fig. 190). The cut on the genuine title is possibly one of the devices used by Mey, but is certainly not a representation of the Arms of the Archbishop, which appear in the faked title given by Arco, and which did in fact appear on the title-page of the same Author's *Juris Pontificii veteris epitome*, which Mey printed in the same year and a copy of which I have in my collection. The *Dialogos de medallas* is an exceedingly well-printed book, and at the end are to be found twenty-six full-page engraved plates of medals, and one of various sized circles, apparently for measurement with each circle designated by a letter of the Greek alphabet. These plates are exceptionally well executed and far in advance of the ordinary work of the period. The book proved a popular one, several editions appearing in Italian at Rome,

[1] Angel del Arco y Molinero, *La Imprenta en Tarragona*, Tarragona, 1916, (p. 436).

besides other editions at Antwerp and Madrid in the seventeenth and eighteenth centuries.   In the Madrid edition of 1744, edited by Dr. Andrés González de Barcia Carballido, he speaks of the great scarcity of examples of the first edition of 1587, and of the trouble he had experienced in obtaining a copy, and then, only one without the engraved plates.   However, later on he was more successful, and reproductions of the plates appear in his edition of 1744.   There are two copies of this edition of 1587 in the British Museum, one of them being imperfect.   My own copy is of special association interest and merits some particulars. Bound in old French olive-green morocco, it bears on its covers the Arms in gold of Aymar du Périer, Conseiller au Parlement de Grenoble, a French Antiquary, who flourished at the end of the sixteenth century.   The copy afterwards belonged to that celebrated scholar, Hadrian Beverland, and his autograph, "Hadriani Beverlandi Oxoniae, 1691," is on the blank margin of the title-page.   On the flyleaf he has also written a note, "Hic liber est omnium rarissimus," and he goes on to say that he acquired it "a Littleburio Londini 50 scill. 1688."   Robert Littlebury, from whom it was thus bought for fifty shillings, was a London bookseller, whose stock was sold by auction at " Tom's Coffee Shop adjoining Ludgate " in 1696.   Pepys, the Diarist, under the date of 16th March of that year, commissions the famous (or to some infamous) [1] Bagford to make a purchase for him at this Sale.[2]

This copy has two impressions of Hadrian Beverland's fine old armorial ex-libris, besides others of Louis Jobert (1647-1719),

[1] John Bagford (1650-1715), a shoemaker by trade, gave up this occupation to purchase books on commission for wealthy patrons, and formed himself an enormous collection of title-pages and other specimens of typography which is now in the British Museum and of inestimable value to the student of early printing.   It is quite doubtful whether he ever destroyed perfect copies to obtain these specimens, and a good deal of the criticism which has been made against him is absolute nonsense.

[2] In the letter, which is in the British Museum, Pepys asks Bagford to look out for a copy of the last edition of *Stoboei Sententiae*, "a fair one for me, so as I may be eased of the charge of its re-binding " !

a subsequent owner of the book and himself a learned Jesuit, and the author of *La science des Medailles*. Later on the copy was in the Blenheim collection.

Felipe Roberto at the end of the century produced several crudely illustrated books of a popular description. For example, *La General Historia del enforçat cavaller Partinobles* in 1588, and an edition of *Celestina* in 1595. The cuts in both these books are of the chap-book variety.

ZAMORA.

If Zamora in the fifteenth century produced the first book with illustrations by a native artist printed in Spain, in the shape of Villena's *Los trabajos de Hercules*, which Antonio Centenera printed in 1483 (see p. 7), the town would seem to have exhausted itself in the effort. Of the work of the subsequent printers there is little or nothing to register in the way of illustrated books. A possible exception may be made in regard to the editions of *Los quatro libros primeros de la Chronica general de España* of Florian de Ocampo, printed in 1541, 1542 and 1543. The first two were the work of Augustin de Paz and Juan Picardo. The 1543 edition was the work of Picardo alone. This 1543 edition is a finely printed book, and the woodcut Arms of Spain on the title an effective and decorative piece of work.

I have an edition in quarto of this Chronicle, which is probably the second edition actually published, but owing to the unfortunate absence of the colophon leaf, one can only conjecture that the book was printed in this town. The printers, in a note addressed to their readers, state that they are issuing the book " en forma mas pequeña, emēdandole de todos vicios que de la primera impression faco, como entendemos hazer en todos los libros que de nuestra casa salieren." The remark about the size is a reference to the fact that the first edition was in folio, while their anxiety to stress the absence of errors from the books issued from their press, is an early and interesting example of advertising enterprise. This copy of mine was formerly in the possession of Richard Heber, who has written a long note on the inside vellum cover, in which he deplores the absence of the final leaf, discusses other editions, and states that he has never seen another copy of this one. The title-page is quite a respectable piece of work, and is here reproduced (Fig. 191), in the hope that it may lead to the discovery of a complete copy of the book. Ocampo's Chronicle is of American interest, and Harrisse (*Bibliotheca Americana Vetustissima*, No. 242), in discussing the 1543 edition, which he calls "an extremely well-printed book," draws attention to the interesting chapter devoted to the discovery of the Islands of Hispaniola, Cuba, etc.

We have now dealt with the sixteenth-century work in all the towns included in our fifteenth-century survey in Part I. There are four other towns, where presses were at work in the fifteenth century, but where, as far as illustrated books were concerned, nothing was produced which required our attention. We will now glance at the sixteenth-century output in these particular towns, and deal with them in the chronological order in which their first presses were established.

TORTOSA.

In the fifteenth century, Pedro Brun and Nicolas Spindeler are credited with two books at this town, one of which I think was probably printed at Barcelona, and neither of which were illustrated. The only printer in the sixteenth century was Arnaldus Guillermus de Monte Pesato. Montpesat is a small French town in the Garonne district. Nothing is previously known about this printer, but his first book at Tortosa in 1538 is of some interest. It is a *Mariale ; de laudibus Beatae virginis sermones* of Balthasar Sorio, who was a Dominican and Rector of the College at Tortosa founded by the Emperor, Charles V. This is a rare book, which is referred to at length by Deschamps, and by Cotton, who mentions that there is a copy in the Library

FIG. 191.—Florian de Ocampo—*Los Quatro Libros Primeros de la Cronica general de España* [Zamora, Augustin de Paz y Juan Picardo, *c.* 1542].

of Trinity College, Dublin.   There is another copy in the British Museum, besides the one in the writer's collection.   The cut on the title-page, which is reproduced (Fig. 192), had already appeared in a *Missale Benedictinum*, printed by Juan Rosembach, *c.* 1521.   It is found again in the *De puerorum moribus disticha* of

FIG. 192.—Sorio—*Mariale*, Tortosa, Arnaldus Guillermus de Monte Pesato, 1538.

Michael Verinus, also printed by Rosembach at Barcelona in 1526, in which book the block is in better condition than in the *Mariale*, where it shows traces of wear.   Initial letters appearing in this book are also to be found in the *Ordinarium Tarraconense* (see p. 56), the last book known to have been printed by Rosembach at Barcelona.

Again, a large full-page cut of the Virgin, which appears on the verso of the title of the *Mariale*, had appeared on the title of the *Missale de Tortosa* which Rosembach had printed at Barcelona in 1524.[1]

This *Mariale* gives us another interesting example of the way in which the material of one printer is found years afterwards in the possession of another printer in a different town. We can leave Arnaldus Guillermus de Monte Pesato with the reflexion that if he was unable, or unwilling, to get fresh illustrations made for his books, he had the supreme good sense to go to the work of a master of the craft when he had occasion to borrow.[2]

[1] For a reproduction of this cut, see *Bibliofilia* (vol. i., p. 334a).

[2] It is possible that the printer of this book was a son of Pedro Mompezat, who received some printing materials from Juan Rosembach for services rendered. (See Konrad Haebler, *Geschichte des spanischen Frühdruckes in Stammbäumen* (p 152), Leipzig, 1923.)

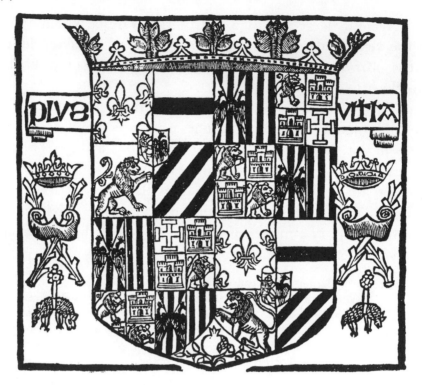

℄Pratica delas virtudes delos bue
nos reyes despaña en coplas de arte
mayor derecadas al esclarecido rey dõ
Carlos nuestro señor.

FIG. 193.—Francisco de Castilla—*Pratica de las virtudes de los buenos reyes despaña,*
Murcia, Gorge Costilla, 1518.
(Reduced, original 238 × 138 mm.)

CHAPTER XIV.

LÉRIDA, MURCIA AND GRANADA.

LÉRIDA is of almost negligible importance from our point of view. Henrique Botel, the fifteenth-century printer, apparently only produced one book in the town, in 1491, in which there was any pretence at decoration. It was a *Bula de indulgencias* (en Catalán), in favour of the Monastery of Coday, in which there is a cut of the Papal Arms of Innocent VIII. (Haebler, 111 (4)). In the sixteenth century, the family of Robles, Pedro de Robles in particular, did most of the printing. He was responsible for some liturgical books, notably a *Ritual Ilerdense* of 1567, which is a nicely printed book, with some decoration and music printed in red and black. I have a copy of the *Orlando determinado* of Martin Bolea y Castro, printed in 1578, on the title-page of which there is a conventional cut of a mounted Knight, in which the rider and the horse are adorned with perhaps more than the usual amount of plumed feathers. The book itself, a poem of chivalry in octaves, is of some rarity, there being no copy in the Salvá collection, while Ticknor states that he had never been able to see one. The British Museum is also without a copy.

MURCIA.

There was only one printer at this town in the fifteenth century, Lope de la Roca, who printed four books, none of which are illustrated. In the sixteenth century the record of typographical activity was even less, as we only find two books recorded, both written by Francisco de Castilla and printed by Gorge de Costilla, the well-known printer at Valencia.

These books (both in folio) are (1) *Theorica de virtudes en coplas de arte humilde con comento* (the last four leaves consist of the *Inquisiciō de la felicidad por metaphora*), which the colophon tells us, " Fue impresso el presente tratado/en la muy noble y leal ciudad de mur/cia. por el honorable Gorge costilla/Acabose a, iiii dias del mes de Ago = /sto año de mil y D.y.xviii años."/ and (2) *Pratica de las virtudes de los bue/nos reyes despaña en coplas de arte/mayor dereçadas al esclarecido rey dō/Carlos nuestro señor.*, which has the following colophon : " A honor y gloria de dios todo/poderoso : y de la sacratissima virgen maria/madre suya y Señora nuestra. Fue impresso/el presente tratado en la muy noble y leal ciudad de Murcia./Por el honorable Gor/ge costilla. Acabose a xx. dias del mes de Ene/ro año de mil y D.y. xviii. años./"

In this second tract, the historical account in verse of the reigns of Ferdinand and Isabella, contains the following interesting reference to the discovery of America, which appears to have escaped the attention of Harrisse :—

> " Ganaron las islas que son de canaria
> Ganaron las indias del mar oceano
> do carga de oro cunado y en grano
> y aljofar y perlas su flota ordinaria.
> Mi breve escritura succincta y sumaria
> No sufre que haga mayor relacion
> de reyes que llevan delantel guion
> su firme ventura que nunca fue varia."

This octave follows others in which the conquest of the Moors, the siege and capture of Granada, and the investments of Oran and Bujía, are all recounted. These treatises, folio in size,[1] are printed in a fine Gothic type, and the decoration of the title-pages, with their unusual form of the Royal Arms, are striking pieces of work.

The title-page of the *Pratica de las virtudes de los buenos reyes despaña* is here reproduced (Fig. 193), as is also the device of the printer (Fig. 194), which is the same as he used at Valencia.

---

[1] The collations are as follow : (1) 38 ff., a-e6, f4, a4. (2) 16 ff. a-b6, c4.

These two solitary productions from the printing press at Murcia in the sixteenth century, were found bound up with an edition of the *Speculum vite humane* of Rodericus Zamorensis, printed in 1507 by Johann Prüss, the Strassburg printer. The books were bound in the original old calf over wooden boards. On the inside of the lower cover, a previous owner had written :

Fig. 194.—Francisco de Castilla—*Pratica de las virtudes de los buenos reyes despaña,*
Murcia, Gorge Costilla, 1518.
(Device of printer.)

" compre este libro en Valladolid siendo conventual en San Pablo Año 1522. Costome siete Reales sin el tratado de Romāce el que me dio el auctor del el señor dō Francisco de Castilla," from which it would appear that he had paid 7 reales for the *Speculum vite humane*, but that the Murcia books had been presented to him by the author.

The present owner would wish that the volume had been

acquired by him on similar advantageous terms, but so called "Americana" is ever regarded by the bookseller from an entirely distorted perspective, as far as price is concerned.

GRANADA.

There are only two books registered as having been printed in this town in the fifteenth century. They were both printed by Juan Pegnitzer and Meinardo Ungut, and neither of them contain any illustrations. The first sixteenth-century printer at work in the town was Juan Varela de Salamanca, whose *Rationale divinorum officiorum* of Guilielmus Durandus was the first book printed in Granada in this century. The only perfect copy that seems to have survived was in the Fairfax Murray collection and is now in mine. An imperfect one, with 242 out of the 278 leaves which the book contains, was sold by Mr. P. M. Barnard some years ago and is now in the collection of my friend, Mr. Stephen Gaselee. The severely simple, but entirely adequate title-page of this folio volume (Fig. 195), the fine crucifixion cut (Fig. 196), the imposing representation of the Royal Arms on the last leaf (Fig. 197), together with some well-designed woodcut capitals, combine, with the careful press-work and handsome Gothic type, to give us one of the best examples of book production in Spain at the beginning of the sixteenth century.

In the next year, 1505, Juan de Varela produced an edition of *Las CCC. del famosissimo poeta juan de mena cō glosa*. This title, which occupies the whole of the page, is a fine piece of xylographic printing, and is from the same block as used in the first edition (with the gloss of Nunez) printed at Seville by the Compañeros Alemanes in 1499 (Haebler, 414), a copy of which is in my possession. The beautiful device of Varela is here reproduced (Fig. 198). He would seem to have worked in Granada during 1504 and 1505, and to have printed not more than three or four books.[1] There is an interval until 1518, when

[1] For the work of Varela at Seville, see p 182.

we find another printer, Andres de Burgos, with a press in this town.   Mention has already been made (see p. 88) of his edition of Livy's *Las Decadas* at Burgos in 1505, and we now

FIG. 195.—Durandus—*Rationale divinorum officiorum*, Granada, Juan Varela de Salamanca, 1504.

find him during 1518 and 1519 at Granada producing two or three medical books.   The one of outstanding interest and importance is the first Spanish edition (hitherto unrecorded) of the

FIG. 196.—Durandus—*Rationale divinorum officiorum*, Granada, Juan Varela de
Salamanca, 1504.
(Reduced, original 224 × 141 mm.)

FIG. 197—Durandus—*Rationale divinorum officiorum*, Granada, Juan Varela de
Salamanca, 1504.
(Reduced, original 229 × 152 mm.)

Thesoro de los Pobres, with Villanova's *Regimiento de sanidad*, which was printed on the 25th of January, 1519. It is described in the colophon as " obra muy provechosa en medicina y cirurgia, jamas imprimida." It is of interest to note that in the " Prologo," the reigning monarchs of Spain are described as " los muy altos y catholicos reyes, la reyna doña Juana : y el rey don Carlos su hijo," which illustrates the reluctance of the Spaniards to ignore

FIG. 198.—Juan de Mena—*Las CCC.*, Granada, Juan Varela, 1505.
(Device of printer.)

the claims of the ill-fated " Juana la loca," as the premier reigning sovereign. The *Thesoro de los Pobres* was an " Everyman his own doctor " of the beginning of the sixteenth century. In printed form it first appeared in the fifteenth century (Hain, 8711-8716). Up to the time of my discovery of this Spanish edition of 1519, one which appeared in Seville in 1543 was supposed to have been the first printed in Spain, and is cited by Escudero, on the authority of Sr. D. Gayangos, but without any description, or particulars. The

1519 edition is in folio, and the title (xylographic) is printed in red.   Above the words of the title is a cut of the Arms of Ant. de Rojas, Archbishop of Granada, surrounded by four small

FIG. 199.—Juliano—*Thesoro de los Pobres*, Granada, Andres de Burgos, 1519.

compartment cuts, representing King David, St. Barbara and St. Peter.   One of these is here reproduced (Fig. 199), and I think it is copied from a cut in the *Tesoro de la pasion* of Andres de Li,

FIG. 200.—Juliano—*Thesoro de los Pobres*, Granada, Andres de Burgos, 1519.

printed by Pablo Hurus at Zaragoza in 1494 (Haebler, 200). On the last leaf, above the colophon, are two pleasing little cuts, white on a black background, one representing a man with a wooden leg (Saturn ?), and the other of a lady playing a stringed instrument (Venus ?).   These two cuts (Figs. 200 and 201) are reproduced. We shall come across another edition of this work when we come to discuss the books printed at Alcalá.

The next printer in this town, Sancho Lebrija (Xanthus Nebrissensis), was a son of Aelius Antonius Nebrissensis, the famous grammarian, historian and scholar. This press, "apud inclytam Granatam," was no doubt established mainly for the purpose of producing editions of his Father's works. In his well-executed and decorated books, he did full and filial justice to the literary productions of his distinguished Father. As an example, his *Rerum a Fernando & Elisabe Hispaniarū foelicissimis Regibus*

FIG. 201.—Juliano—*Thesoro de los Pobres*, Granada, Andres de Burgos, 1519.

gestar., printed, as he tells us in his Preface, "Ex officina nostra literaria apud inclytam Granatam," is a magnificently decorated and printed book. There are three works in the volume, each with a separate title-page, and all three are dated 1545. These titles are fine pieces of decorative work, as will be seen from the reproduction of the *Episcopi Gerundensis Paralipomenon Hispaniae* (Fig. 202). In the border of this title, and also in the printer's device (Fig. 203), will be found a curious mark, in the shape of a capital Y, which has given rise to a good deal of conjecture. It has been said to be merely a letter of the alphabet, but some think it to be the symbol of wisdom in the system of Pythagoras,

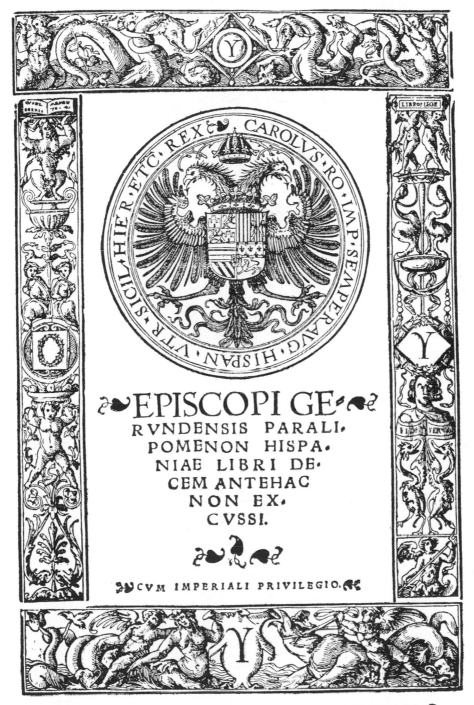

FIG. 202.—Nebrissensis—*Rerum a Fernando & Elisabe*, Granada, 1545.
(Reduced, original 241 × 157 mm.)

while others say that it is in fact a representation of a tool or instrument in common use in the establishments of the early

FIG. 203.—Nebrissensis—*Rerum a Fernando & Elisabe*, Granada, 1545. (Device of printer.)

printers.   The woodcut capitals throughout the book are above the average, as will be seen from the one here reproduced (Fig.

FIG. 204.—Nebrissensis—*Rerum a Fernando & Elisabe*, Granada, 1545.

204).   This book is scarce in a complete form, as each of the three parts which it contains had been separately issued.

Hugo Mena, the last printer whose work need detain us at Granada, worked for upwards of forty years during the second half of the century.   His *Carmina* (and other works) of Juan de Latino, which he printed in 1573, is a fine piece of work, the italic type used, and the general scheme of decoration, combin-

FIG. 205.—Juan de Latino—*Carmina*, Granada, Hugo Mena, 1573.

ing to produce a most pleasing result.   A small crucifixion cut from this book is here reproduced (Fig. 205).

We now propose to deal with some of the more important of those towns where no printing press at all had been in operation until the sixteenth century. We shall treat them in chronological order, and briefly review the output at Alcalá, Logroño, Medina del Campo, Segovia, Cuenca, Astorga, Madrid, Antiquera, Bilbao and Malaga.

FIG. 206.—*Biblia Complutense*, Alcalá, A. G. de Brocar, 1517.
(Reduced, original 264 × 188 mm.)

CHAPTER XV.

ALCALÁ DE HENARES.

IT is fitting that our consideration of the purely sixteenth-century presses should commence with this town, which from every point of view is one of the most interesting in the history of book production in this century. Any review of the illustrated books which were printed at Alcalá must necessarily only be a brief attempt to select some of its representative printers and give examples of their work.

Alcalá de Henares (the "Castle on the river") had as its old Roman name "Complutum," or the meeting-place of two rivers. A town memorable in Spanish history, it was the birth-place of Queen Catherine of Aragon, and also of Miguel de Cervantes Saavedra. The site of the famous University, founded by Cardinal Ximenes de Cisneros, it is not very surprising that the printing press was a flourishing, and not inconsiderable part of the town's activities during this century.

Reference has already been made (see p. 68) to its first printer, Stanislao Polono, and to the very notable example of early printing, which he produced here in 1502. He ceased to print at Alcalá in 1504.

The printer whose name will ever be associated with the typographical history of Alcalá, was Arnaldo Guillen de Brocar, who in all probability originally came from the South of France. He is first found in Pamplona in 1489, where he printed some sixteen books before the end of the fifteenth century. In 1503, as we shall see later, he was at Logroño, and his activities at Toledo have been already mentioned (see p. 222). There is very

(259)

little doubt that Brocar was brought to Alcalá by Cardinal Ximenes, but be that as it may, we find him from 1511 onwards

FIG. 207.—*Biblia Complutense*, Alcalá, A. G. de Brocar, 1514.
(Reduced, original 285 × 180 mm.)

printing and publishing books under the patronage and direction of that famous ecclesiastic and man of letters.

The book upon which Brocar's undying fame as a printer will always rest, was the *Biblia Complutense*, or the well-known

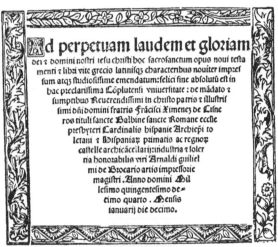

FIG. 208.—*Biblia Complutense*, Alcalá, A. G. de Brocar, 1514.
(Reduced, original 283 × 179 mm.)

Complutensian Polyglot Bible. I have told elsewhere in full detail the history of this wonderful work.[1] It is certainly no

[1] Lyell, *Cardinal Ximenes . . . with an Account of the Complutensian Polyglot Bible*, London, Grafton & Co., 1917.

exaggeration to describe it as one of the monuments of early typography in Spain. The reproductions of the decorative work of Brocar in this book consist of (*a*) The special form of Old Testament title-page (Fig. 206), (*b*) The New Testament title-page (Fig. 207), (*c*) The N.T. colophon and Brocar's device (Fig. 208), and (*d*) as a true example of artistic book decoration which it would be very difficult to equal, a specimen of the wonderful fount of Greek type (Fig. 209). Robert Proctor has said [1] of this type, "To Spain belongs the honour of having produced as her first Greek type, what is undoubtedly the finest

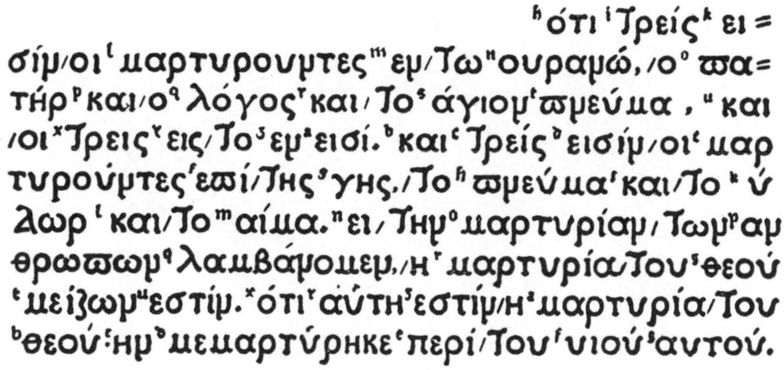

ᵇότι ¹Τρεὶς ᵏ ει =
σίμ/οι⁴μαρτυρουμτες ᵐεμ/Τω ⁿουραμώ,/οᵒ ϖα=
τήρ ᵖκαι/οᵠ λόγος ⁴και/Το³ άγιομ ⁴ϖρεύμα , ⁴και
/οι ˣΤρεις ˣεις/Το³εμ ⁴εισί. ᵇκαι ⁴Τρείς ᵇεισίμ/οι⁴μαρ
τυρούμτες ⁴εϖί/Της ⁹γης,/Το ʰ ϖμεύμα ⁴και/Το ᵏ ύ
Δωρ ¹και/Το ᵐ αίμα. ⁿει/Τημ ᵒμαρτυρίαμ/Τωρ ᵖαμ
θρωϖωρ ⁴λαμβάμομεμ,/ἡ ⁴μαρτυρίαΤου ⁴θεού
⁴μείзωμ ᵘεστίμ. ˣότι ⁴αύτη ⁴εστίμ/ἡ ⁴μαρτυρία/Του
ᵇθεού ᶜημ ᵇμεμαρτύρηκε ⁴περί/Του ⁴υιού ⁴αυτού.

FIG. 209.—*Biblia Complutense*, Alcalá, A. G. de Brocar, 1514.

Greek fount ever cut." This type is singularly simple and beautiful, and Brocar himself tells us in his preface that it was cut after the model of a Greek manuscript lent to Cardinal Ximenes by Pope Leo X.

Brocar employed as his device three varieties in the six-folio volumes of this Bible. We have already seen the small one, which follows the N.T. colophon. It consists of a circle, printer's staff and monogram, in white on a black background. The one at the end of the O.T. is within a woodcut border and measures, including the border, 185 × 147 mm.

[1] Proctor, *The Printing of Greek in the Fifteenth Century*, Bib. Soc. Monograph, 1900.

The device itself (125 × 80 mm.) represents a figure kneeling before the Cross. There are portrait medallions of two
Saints, one in each of the top corners ; below, there are two

Explicit quarta et vltima pars totius veteris testaméti be-
braico grecoꝗ et latino idiomate nunc primū impressa in hac preclarissima Complutensi
vniuersitate. De mandato ac sumptibus Reuerendissimi in christo patris & domi
ni:domini. F. Francisci Ximenez de Cisneros tituli Sancte Balbine sacro
sancte Romane ecclesie presbyteri Cardinalis Hispanie Archiepisco
pi Toletani & hispaniarum primatis : ac regnorum castelle
Archicancellarii. Industria & solertia honorabilis
viri Arnaldi Guillelmi de Brocario artis impres
sorie Magistri. Anno Domini Mille
simo qngētesimo decimo se
ptimo. mēsis Iulii die
decimo.

Que in hoc volumine continentur hec sunt.
Esaias. Hieremias. Threni. Baruch. Ezechiel. Daniel. Osee. Iohel. Amos. Abdias.
Ionas. Micheas. Naum. Abachuc. Sophonias. Aggeus. Zacharias. Malachias. Macha
beorum primus. Machabeorum secundus, Machabeorum tertius.

FIG. 210.—*Biblia Complutense*, Alcalá, A. G. de Brocar, 1517.
(Reduced, original 279 × 170 mm.)

figures upon pedestals upholding a triangle, within which is the motto, " In hoc signo vinces." At the foot his initials appear in monogram (Fig. 210). The same device appears at the end of the Vocabulary volume, but with a different motto, viz. : " Per signū Cru/cis de inimi/cis nr̄is libera/nos dñe Deus/noster."

The relations between Cardinal Ximenes and Brocar were of the friendliest description, and we are told that when Brocar's son (Juan de Brocar) carried the last sheets of this Bible to the aged Cardinal, then lying on his death-bed, that raising his eyes to heaven, the old man exclaimed, " I give Thee thanks, O most High God, that Thou hast brought to the long-wished-for end this book which I undertook."

Of Brocar's other work, mention may be made of *Las Epistolas y Oraciones* of St. Catherine of Sienna, printed in 1512, where the Arms of Cardinal Ximenes add dignity to the title-page (Fig. 211). The *De Senectute, De Amicicia, De Republica and Paradoxa* of Cicero, which he printed *c.* 1516, has his large device which he used in the Old Testament volume of the Complutensian Polyglot Bible, but with a different motto, which now reads : " Nos aūt gloriari oportet/in cruce dñi nr̄i iesu/xp̄i. Dulce lignū/dulces clavos/dulcia ferēs pōdera." This device we have already noted as having been used by Brocar at Toledo in 1520 in his *Sedulii paschale cū cōmento Antonii Nebrissen,* (see p. 223), but in the Cicero, the last word in the motto has been abbreviated from " pondera " to " pōdera." This edition of Cicero would seem to be the earliest one of any of his works printed in Spain. The only recorded copy, other than the one in my collection, is in the Biblioteca de San Isidro. The book is printed in *letra transicion* and has some woodcut capitals. Another of this printer's books of great rarity is the *Epistola Ferdinandi de Enzinas,* printed in 1524. A treatise dealing with the astronomical views and contentions of Albert Pighius, it is dedicated to " Ferdinādo de Aragonia Calabrie duci," and on the last leaf, within ornamental borders, is another, and perhaps the most decorative device of Brocar. At the top, there is the man kneeling at the Cross, while underneath, there are two angels holding up

Obra delas epistolas y oraciones de la bien auenturada virgen sancta catherina de sena dela orde delos predicadores. Las quales fue ron traduzidas ol toscano en nuestralengua castellana por mandado del muy Illustre y Reuerēdissimo señor el Carde nal despaña Arcobispo dela sancta yglesia de Toledo. rc.

Con preuilegio real.

FIG. 211.—S. Catherina de Sena—*Las Epistolas*, Alcalá, A. G. de Brocar, 1512.
(Reduced, original 214 × 135 mm.)

a shield, within which is his monogram surmounted by a porcupine (Fig. 212). There is also this strange motto : " Inimici hominis domestici ejus." It has been suggested that we have here an indication of family dissension, or possibly some reflexion upon the competency of his workpeople, but it is a motto which has never been satisfactorily explained. Garcia (No. 68) cites this book, but cannot give the whereabouts of any existing copy. It presents an example of the rhyming colophon which runs :—

> "Hoc opus impressum Compluti suspici lector :
> Arnaldo et grates qui tibi pressit ages." [1]

Brocar's work at Alcalá was characterised by originality and competent workmanship. The decoration, considering the class of literature associated with the University and ecclesiastical atmosphere of the town at the time, was wholly adequate and suitable. As far as illustrated books were concerned, he left them severely alone. The patronage of a Cardinal would seem to have forbidden any attempt to give pictorial assistance to the reader, in marked contradistinction to his work at Logroño, where he produced at least one finely illustrated book under the less austere supervision of an Emperor.

The next printer who calls for notice is Miguel de Eguia. It was no doubt difficult to follow a man like Brocar, and to uphold the traditions which that master had established. On the whole, Eguia worthily sustained the reputation of his predecessor. In the selection from his books which we will now proceed to discuss, it will be seen how progressively he sought to improve the artistic standard of his decorative work.

His books were also characterised by careful attention to press work and a regard for the quality of the paper employed. In an edition of Pulgar's *Los claros Varones del España*, which

---

[1] Pighius, whose astronomical theories are faithfully dealt with by the author of this book, wrote the *De ratione Paschalis celebrationis*, which, printed in Paris in 1520, contains a reference to "the new land lately discovered by Vespuccius under the auspices of the most Christian King of Spain and which, on account of its magnitude, has been called the New World, is known by the observation of Vespuccius to extend further than 35 degrees beyond the Equator, and the end of it has not yet been found."

he produced in 1526, he places the title within borders consisting of ornamental pillars, which give a dignified and impressive

FIG. 212.—*Epistola, Ferdinandi de Enzinas,* Alcalá, A. G. de Brocar, 1524.
(Device of printer.)

appearance to the page, the result of its entire simplicity and severity of treatment. In the choice of woodcut initial letters, we begin to see the glimmering of an attempt to make these, not merely a decorative, but a harmonious part of the printed page. Some of them in this particular book, white floral decoration on a black background, are very effective. Salvá and Garcia both describe this edition as very rare, and neither of them are able to cite the whereabouts of a copy.

Among the authors to whose works Eguia seems to have devoted special attention was Pedro Ciruelo, eight of whose books he printed between 1520 and 1528. Ciruelo was a mathematician, astrologer, philosopher and ecclesiastic, and if we take as an example of Eguia's work at this period the *Expositio Libri Missalis*, printed in February 1528, it must not be forgotten that the author, a distinguished alumnus of the University of Alcalá, gained his literary reputation more in the field of science than of theology.

This *Expositio Libri Missalis* is a handsome folio volume, the title mainly printed in red and within borders composed of twelve separate compartment cuts, each of which contains a portrait of some Evangelist, Saint, or other Father of the Church. On the verso of this title, there is a large cut within borders, occupying the whole page, in which the Virgin is depicted in company with St. Ildefonso. On the recto of the last leaf, there is a full-page cut of a large plum tree (ciruelo), being the Arms adopted by the author as a play upon his name. There are a number of large and small woodcut capitals, decorative in character, and of more than usual artistic merit. The plum tree device had appeared in other works of Ciruelo and is here reproduced (Fig. 213). My copy of the book bears the autograph of Juan de Castellanos on the blank margin of the title. He was the well-known ecclesiastic of New Granada, who wrote the famous *Elegias de varones Illustres de Indias* in 1589, in which he recounts in verse the doings of Columbus and the other discoverers of America.   No doubt the copy of the *Expositio Libri Missalis* had been in his possession when he was a student at the

FONS · SᴀPIEN·

Cᴕᴏ̃feſſionario del maeſtro Pedro círuelo: nueuamẽte coꝛregido.

Fɪɢ. 213.—P. Ciruelo—*Confesonario*, Alcalá, Miguel de Eguia, 1524.

University of Alcalá, where the book was printed.   It is of interest in this connexion to note that Eguia in his colophon describes himself " in aedibus Michaelis de Eguia Bibliographi," a description which he no doubt considered was in keeping with his surroundings. We find him in 1529 printing two books, which illustrate the improvement in his decorative work. The *Epistolas de Seneca en Romance* has a title-page within a border of compartment cuts, consisting of portraits and legends of the

FIG. 214.—*Epistolas de Seneca*, Alcalá, Miguel de Eguia, 1529.
(Reduced, original 222 × 146 mm.)

Ancients. At the foot, two of the cuts have a monogram, which make up the name "Pedro" (Fig. 214). The other book, the *Commentarios de Cayo Julio Cesar*, published on 1st August, 1529, presents a type of decorative title-page, in which there is quite an unusual amount of detail. It consists of compartment cuts, representing the labours of Hercules (Fig. 215). This is the

FIG. 215.—*Commentarios de Cayo Julio Cesar*, Alcalá, Miguel de Eguia, 1529.

second edition of Cæsar's Commentaries in Spanish, the first having been printed at Toledo in 1498 (Haebler, 113). In the following year (1530), we find Eguia using this elaborate border again in the *De Orbe Novo* of Peter Martyr, which was the first complete edition of his eight Decades, and one of the very important early works concerning America. In May, 1536, the *Tratado de Re Militari* of Diego de Salazar was issued, "en casa de Miguel de Eguia." Whether he was personally responsible for its production I do not know, but the title-page, printed in red and black, with a cut of the Arms of Diego de Vargas y Carvajal, is an indifferent piece of work, and the cuts and diagrams throughout the book, which illustrate military dispositions and formations, are certainly of more interest to the soldier than to the student of early woodcuts.

Juan de Brocar, who commenced to print about 1538, and who worked until his death in 1552, was a prolific printer, who produced a very large number of books at this town. A son of Arnaldo Guillen de Brocar, we have already referred to his visit to Cardinal Ximenes with the last sheets of the Complutensian Polyglot Bible. There is no doubt that he had been trained in his Father's printing office. A writer and a student, as well as a printer, we shall not be far wrong in conjecturing that the delay in taking up the work of the printing press after his Father's death was due to his literary studies. In 1539, we find him publishing *Las cosas memorables de España* of Lucio Marineo Siculo. The title-page, with its architectural and emblematical borders, enclosing a well-executed cut of the Royal Arms, is a good piece of work. The book, which is very well printed, has also a number of woodcut capitals of some merit. It has American interest, as among other references to the New World we find in a chapter headed, "De otras Yslas apartadas del Hemispherio llamadas Indias," Columbus called for the first time "Pedro Colon," and the fact disputed that he was the first discoverer of America. In 1541, the *Rhetorica en lengua Castellana,* attributed to Miguel de Salinas, appeared from Brocar's press. A beautifully printed book, quarto in size, it has a title in red and

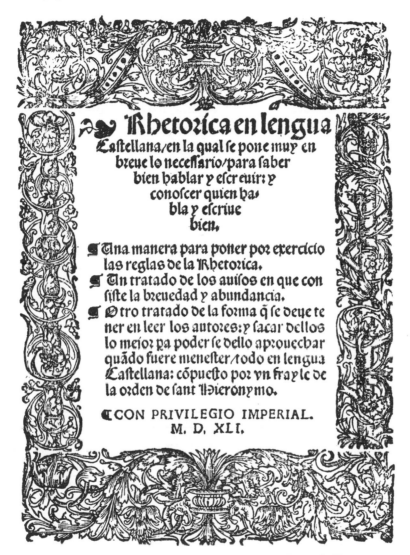

FIG. 216.—*Rhetorica en lengua Castellana*, Alcalá, Juan de Brocar, 1541. (Reduced, original 183 × 127 mm., printed in red and black.)

black, within borders (Fig. 216), and the Arms of Spain on the verso, similarly enclosed. A book of considerable interest, and one which Fernandez, in his description of the Alcalá books in

the Library of the Escorial, describes as " esta obra rara y preciosa." In December, 1543, Brocar printed the first edition of the
Aviso de Caçadores y de Caça of Nuñez de Avendaño, one of the
early Spanish books on hunting and the chase. On the title
there is a cut of the Arms of Inigo Lopez de Mendoza between
two columns. A very well-designed cut of the author's Arms
appears on fol. 43 b, and a series of good woodcut capitals, good
printing and paper, all unite to make this a pleasing specimen
of the printer's art. In his colophon, Brocar pays tribute to the
town and University in the words : " Imp̄sso en la muy noble
villa y florētissima Universidad de Alcalá de Henares."

The *Obras q̄ Francisco Cervantes de Salazar ha hecho*, which
he printed in 1546, has three decorative title-pages in red and
black, within borders, while his device (Fig. 217), representing
the Devil, a Knight and a Lady, is an intriguing piece of work.
Salvá (No. 3869) speaks of this book as "magnificamente impresos " and "mui rara." The author was a contemporary of
Hernando Cortes, the Conqueror of Mexico, and the discoverer
of California. In a dedication, which he addresses to Cortes,
whom he describes as " Discoverer and Conqueror of New Spain,"
he eulogises him as follows : " In a short time, quicker than
Alexander or Cæsar, you conquered so many thousands of men
and won such a great expanse of territory that not without reason
Geographers call it the New World." Again, he recalls that
" some of the Indians called you Son of the Sun which they
worshipped as their God, others believed that you were some
Spirit come down from Heaven, which was not to be wondered
at, when they saw on many occasions 500 Spaniards conquer
100,000 Indians."

In this same year, Brocar produced the *Publica Laetitia* of
Alvarez Gomez de Castro, a quarto volume of 74 leaves, printed
in Roman type, with some specimens of Hebrew and Greek.
We have here one of the few examples of an Alcalá book with
a number of cuts. On the title-page, there is a large cut of the

Arms of Siliceus, Archbishop of Toledo, surrounded by his names and rank, with a shield in the centre with the I.H.S. surrounded by flames. On the verso of this leaf, there is another large cut of the Arms of Cardinal Ximenes. At the end of the book, there are a number of remarkable full-page woodcuts, averaging

FIG. 217.—F. Cervantes de Salazar—*Obras*, Alcalá, Juan de Brocar, 1546.
(Device of printer.)

127 × 95 mm., which are emblematic in character and bold in design. One of them is here reproduced (Fig. 218). In addition to the Latin prose and verse, fourteen pages are devoted to poetry in the vernacular, some of it " en Tercetos Castellanos." Like all other early picture books, few copies have survived. There are two in Spanish Libraries, one in the British Museum, and

the one in the writer's possession, which was formerly in the Heber and Britwell Court collections. Heber has written on the flyleaf that he bought it at the sale of the library of Gregorio Mayáns y Siscâr, in March, 1829, for 10s. 6d. in its original

116   PVBLICA LAETITIA

FIG. 218.—Gomez—*Publica Laetitia*, Alcalá, Juan de Brocar [1546].

parchment cover ; that he had paid an additional 1s. 6d. as commission to Thorpe, the bookseller, and that in December, 1832, he had paid Charles Lewis £1 12s. for rebinding it in its present dress of cross-grained green morocco, a total cost of £2 4s., which is all duly noted.

We will conclude our notes on Juan de Brocar's press by referring to the first edition of the *Epistolas Familiares* of Francisco
Ortiz, which he produced in November, 1551. As usual, the title-
page is surrounded by a fine border, and above the words of the
title, there is a well-executed oval cut of the Arms of the Duque
de Medina Celi, whose descendant to-day, has placed all students
of early Spanish printing under such deep obligation, by the
finely printed and illustrated catalogue of the early books and
manuscripts in his own collection. On the verso of the fourth
leaf of the *Epistolas Familiares*, facing the first page of the text,

FIG. 219.—F. Ortiz—*Epistolas Familiares*, Alcalá, Juan de Brocar, 1551.

there is a cut of "Justice" overcoming evil, in the shape of a
prostrate devil, and rewarding good deeds, by placing a coin in
the cap of a man who is kneeling in her path ! One of the
decorative features of the book is a series of large initial letters,
each representing some Biblical subject. One of them, a well-
known incident in the life of Noah, is here reproduced (Fig. 219).

We have touched upon the three chief figures in the typographical history of this town, and only passing reference can be
made to the other printers who occupied the stage during the
last half of the century. Of these, one of the most important
was Andres de Angulo, who printed in 1569 the *De Rebus Gestis*

A Francisco Ximenio Cisnerio, of Alvaro Gomez de Castro, the biographer of the famous Cardinal.   In small folio, it is one of the finest specimens of Roman type of the period.   The title-page,

FIG. 220.—Gomez—*De Rebus Gestis A Francisco Ximenio Cisnerio*, Alcalá, Andres de Angulo, 1569.
(Reduced, original 276 × 195 mm.)

with the Arms of the Cardinal in the centre, is here reproduced (Fig. 220), together with a striking woodcut portrait of the subject of the biography (Fig. 221).   We owe to this book most of the information that is known regarding one of Spain's greatest sons.

The *Libro de la verdad* of Pedro de Medina (the famous author of the *Arte de Navegar*) was printed by Juan de Villanueva in 1568, and is notable for an unusual medallion-

FIG. 221.—Gomez—*De Rebus Gestis A Francisco Ximenio Cisnerio*, Alcalá, Andres de Angulo, 1569.
(Reduced, original 155 × 124 mm.)

shaped woodcut portrait of our Lord, which is found on the title-page.

Sebastian Martinez printed in the same year an edition of the *Libro de Sant Iuan Climaco, Llámado escala spiritual*, translated by Luys de Granada. A small octavo volume, it has a small oval cut on the title (32 × 26), representing a crucifix and church. On the recto of the fourth leaf, there is a full-page cut of the Saint at prayer, surrounded by four disciples (88 × 68 mm.),

Gloſſas y canciones.　　211

ꟿSIGVENSE GLOS

SAS Y CANCIONES DE DIF

ferentes authores, de donde ſacara el

lector mucho auiſo.

Ontentamiento, do eſtas
que no te tiene ninguno?
ſi pienſa tenerte alguno
no ſabe por donde vas.

Gloſſa.

Dd 5　　Con-

FIG. 222.—L. Rodriguez—*Romancero Historiado*, Alcalá, H. Ramirez, 1581.

which has all the appearance of being earlier than the book. This edition seems to be unrecorded and has escaped the attention of Garcia. Martinez was also responsible for two editions of well-known works, the first was the *Thesoro de los Pobres*, the rare first Spanish edition of which at Granada we have already noticed (see p. 252). This Alcalá edition of 1584, in small octavo, has a cut on the title of Cosme and Damion. The second book, Padilla's *Retablo de la vida de Christo*, in 1588, has a cut on the title of the Crucifixion, besides numerous small cuts in the text. Both these books are rare, but are very badly printed, and on shocking paper. They afford an example of the deterioration in printing which took place at Alcalá, as well as in other towns towards the end of the century.

Juan Iñiguez de Lequeríca, another printer at this town, published in 1577 a *Compendio de algunas historias de España*, by Geronymo Gudiel, which has special reference to the family " de los Girones." It is an important work on Spanish genealogy and history, and contains some forty genealogical trees, some four of them being on large folding plates.

The *Romancero Historiado cō mucha variedad de glossas y sonetos*, which was compiled by Lucas Rodriguez, and printed by Hernan Ramirez at Alcalá in 1581, is a book of extreme rarity. It is full of crude cuts of the chap-book variety, and badly printed on correspondingly bad paper, an explanation no doubt of the scarcity of surviving copies. A page from my copy (formerly in the Yemeniz collection) is here reproduced (Fig. 222). It forms a fitting example of the work produced by the later Alcalá printers.

Speculum sapientie Beati Cirilli epi
alias quadripartitus apologietic⁹ vo
catus. In cuius quidē prouerbijs om
nis Ꝛ totius sapientie speculum claret.

FIG. 223.—Cyrillus—*Speculum*, Logroño, A. G. de Brocar, 1503.

CHAPTER XVI.

LOGROÑO AND MEDINA DEL CAMPO.

ARNALDO GUILLEN DE BROCAR, whose work at Alcalá we have already discussed, was responsible for the first press in Logroño in 1503. In that year he produced the *Liber de oculo morali* of Domingo Ponzon, which has a cut on the title representing a preacher addressing a congregation from the pulpit, which in treatment and in design is not unlike the work of the Florentine woodcutters. In the same year he produced the *Speculum*, of Cyrillus, which has also a cut upon the title, in which a quaint reading desk forms a conspicuous feature (Fig. 223). The only other recorded copy is in the Bib. Columbina. At this time, and at his press in this town, there may be attributed to A. G. de Brocar one of the most interesting examples of the ephemeral productions of the early sixteenth century printing press. It is a single sheet, or broadside, the type measurement of which is 278 × 177 mm., an *Indulgēcia y cofadria del hospital de señor Santiago*, which is here reproduced on a slightly reduced scale (Fig. * 223).[1] The ornamental initial letter with which it opens represents a pilgrim with his staff in his hand, while at the foot of the sheet is a fine woodcut equestrian portrait of St. James, surrounded by a border composed of foliage and the scallop shells, which are the conventional badge of the pilgrim (74 + 62 mm.). Opposite this cut is the woodcut signature of the Administrator of the Hospital, and alongside, there is a well-preserved wax seal covered with paper on the original, which is not shown in the reproduction. The Indulgence is printed in two founts of Gothic letter and consists of 46 lines of type. It was granted by Pope Alexander VI. (Rodrigo Borgia, a member of an old Spanish

[1] Facing p. 101.

(283)

family) to those who contributed to the building of a hospital at Santiago, which Ferdinand and Isabella were erecting according to the plans and design of Enrique de Egas in 1504. This year appears on the Indulgence and it was the same one in which Queen Isabella died. The Indulgence is also expressed to be granted in favour of those who contributed to the maintenance of the pilgrims and the relief of the poor and sick. There is a copy of this Indulgence in Latin in the British Museum (C. 18. e.i. (75)), which bears the date 1503, a year earlier than the present one in the vernacular. It is apparently the only example in our national collection of an early Indulgence printed in Spain, although, as has already been seen, several examples are to be found among Spanish incunabula. (See Figs. 3, 4, 12, and 70.)

Of this Spanish issue of 1504, I can find no other recorded copy, and although it was not until the time of Charles V. that Brocar obtained in 1517 the formal appointment as printer of these Bulls and Indulgences, he had already printed one in Pamplona about the year 1500 (Haebler, 111 *bis*), a copy of which is in the Library of the Escorial. Dr. Haebler tells me that in his opinion this Indulgence in Spanish was printed by Brocar at Logroño, and his view has been confirmed by other expert advice which he has taken. I should have otherwise have been inclined to place it at Toledo or Valladolid. Wherever it was printed and by whom, it forms a remarkable link with the past history of the Spanish people. The town of Santiago, or *Compostella* (campus stellae), is so named after St. James, the Elder, and according to the Spanish legend, based no doubt upon instances which frequently occur in pagan mythology, the body of St. James was taken after his martyrdom at Jerusalem in A.D. 42 in a boat, some say a large scallop shell, from Joppa to Padron close to Santiago, in a period of seven days, which leads Ford to observe that the miracle is obvious, as the steamship company of his time took very much longer! Be all this as it may, Santiago became the Mecca of Spain, and through all the intervening centuries and down to the

present time, a varying stream of pilgrims has visited the town
and its beautiful cathedral, with which is associated the hospital,

FIG. 224.—F. Perez de Guzman—*La cronica del Rey Don Juan II.*, Logroño, A. G.
de Brocar, 1517.
(Reduced, original 269 × 205 mm., printed in red and black.)

a large square building with a chapel in the centre and so
arranged that all the patients can see the service.

In these secular and prosaic days, while we must not scrutinise too closely the details of the original legend, it is refreshing to recall the simple faith which has enabled countless thousands to perform an act of pious pilgrimage in support of their religion and at a very real sacrifice of time, money, and often of physical health.

A well-printed edition of *Aurelii Prudentii Clementis viri consularis Libelli cum cōmento Antonii Nebrissensis*, was printed here by Brocar in 1512. The title-page has a very fine cut of the Royal Arms and one of the printer's smaller devices at the end of the book. Apparently in some copies, a second title-page is found with three additional leaves, consisting of a dedicatory epistle by Nebrissensis to J. Ramirez, in which a slight reference to America has been noted by Harrisse (Adds. No. 44). The work of Brocar in this town ceased in 1517, and he signalised it by the publication of one of the most sumptuously printed of the early Spanish books. It was *La cronica del Rey Don Juan II.*, by Fernan Perez de Guzman. One of the most notable of the Spanish historical classics, Brocar produced it by direct command of the Emperor, Charles V. A large and imposing folio volume, the title-page, printed in red and black, is a fine piece of work. On it appears a cut of a king, seated upon his throne, with two figures kneeling before him, one (presumably the author) engaged in reading out of a book (Fig. 224). The page is surrounded by specially fine borders, white on a black background. On the verso of fol. 10, there is a well-executed crucifixion cut, signed by I.D., one of the master Spanish woodcutters, and one of the few whose work can be definitely identified (Fig. 225). Facing the first page of the text, we find a full-page equestrian portrait of King John II., surrounded by compartment woodcut portraits of Spanish Royalties and other important personages. The book is printed throughout in red and black and has some fine wood-cut capitals. At the end, the colophon, printed entirely in red, is followed by one of Brocar's beautiful devices. It has been suggested that some copies of this book were issued on large

FIG. 225.—F. Perez de Guzman—*La cronica del Rey Don Juan II.*, Logroño, A. G. de Brocar, 1517.
(Reduced, original 268 × 180 mm.)

paper.   I should doubt this, although the copy from which this description is given is a specially large one, with ample margins, which, combined with its original limp vellum binding with ties, affords a superb example of the magnificence of some of the early Spanish books.   Two or three copies of this book were printed on vellum, probably for presentation copies by the Emperor.

The only other printer at Logroño we need mention, is Miguel de Eguia, who, like A. G. de Brocar, migrated from time to time from his headquarters at Alcalá to this town and to Toledo. We will give as an example of his work here the *Libro de las cosas maravillosas* of Marco Polo, translated by Rodrigo de Santaella, the Confessor to Ferdinand and Isabella.   The title-page is a pleasing piece of work (Fig. 226), and there are a number of woodcut capitals throughout the book, which is of American interest. In the " Prologo del Interprete," and the "Cosmographia intro-ductoria," there are some interesting references to the New World.   For example, on fol. 2b, " And whereas many simple people, and even men of some education, believe that Antilla, or the islands which have been recently found under the patronage of our most Catholic King Ferdinand and Queen Isabella, are in the Indies, they are deceived by the fact that the name of Indies has been given to them.   And because gold has been found in Española, some have presumed to say that it is really Tarsis, Ophir and Cethin from which gold was brought in the time of Solomon to Jerusalem, and adding error to error, they presume to say that when the prophets spoke of the name of our Lord to all nations in the most remote parts of the earth, that it is to these Indies they refer."   It was no doubt this passage which inspired Gaspar de Barros to write his famous treatise, *De Orphyra regione*.   As an example of an amusing piece of contem-porary nomenclature, we are told in the Preface that it was cus-tomary to call a negro "Juan Blanco," and a negress " Margarita." Harrisse (Adds. No. 89) calls this the third edition, quoting

FIG. 226.—Marco Polo—*Libro de las cosas maravillosas*, Logroño, Miguel de Eguia, 1529. (Reduced, original 242 × 168 mm.)

previous ones printed by Varela at Seville in 1518 and by Jacobo
Cromberger at the same town two years later. As a matter of
fact, the first Spanish edition of this translation was printed at
Seville by Polonus and Cromberger in 1503, being the first of
some five books for which they were jointly responsible in that
year. It is therefore clear that these references of American
interest are some years earlier than Harrisse had imagined.

MEDINA DEL CAMPO.

The printing press at this town did not make its appearance
until 1511, when Nicolas de Piemonte produced one book, a
Valerio de las historias, which apparently had neither decoration
nor illustrations. It was not until 1534 that the next printer,
Pedro Tobans, printed a book, on the title-page of which, a
bishop, a young man and Satan are the principal figures. He
also produced at this period some romances of chivalry and similar works, the titles of which have some crude cuts. Take, for
an example, the *Cancionero* of Luis de Castillo, which he printed
in 1535, the title-page of which introduces us to four small cuts
of a Knight hiding himself under some trees, a Cupid and a
young couple to complete the picture ! It was not until Pedro
de Castro appeared upon the scene, about 1540, that there was
any book decoration, or illustration of any importance at all.
His *Subida del monte Sion* by Bernardino de Lareda, printed in
November, 1542, is quite an interesting piece of work. The
title, printed in red, is within a woodcut border, the top compartment of which bears the initials I.D.V. (Juan de Vingles).
This border is used in many books by Pedro de Castro and
also by Pierres Tobans at Salamanca. The text is illustrated by
eleven small cuts, some of them on metal. There are also three
large ones, one of which, a Crucifixion, signed with the monogram of Vingles, has been reproduced (Fig. 145). This cut had
previously appeared in an edition of Ciruelo's *Reprovacion de las
Supersticiones*, printed by Pierres Tobans at Salamanca in 1540.

In the *Fuero Real de España* of Alonso Diaz de Montalvo, printed by De Castro in 1544, we have a very characteristic

FIG. 227.—Boscan y Garcilaso—*Las obras*, Medina del Campo, Pedro de Castro, 1544.
(Slightly reduced).

example of his work.   The volume, which is in folio, has a title-page printed in red and black, with an unusual and striking cut of the Royal Arms, white on a black background, which Pérez Pastor reproduces in his bibliography of this town, together with the devices of G. de Millis, the publisher, and De Castro, the printer.[1]   In the same year we find an edition of *Las obras del Boscan* (Fig. 227).

An extremely rare edition of *Amadis de Gaula* was printed " en la noble villa de Medina del cāpo, en compania Joan de villaquiran, y Pedro de castro Impressores.   Acabose primero dia del mes de Deziembre, del año del nascimiento de Jesu Xp̄o. M.d. xlv."   This would seem to be the only recorded book in which Villaquiran and Pedro de Castro were associated together as printers.   It has been suggested that Villaquiran got the commission to print the book, and not wishing to leave his press at Valladolid, left the actual printing of it to De Castro and was content with his own name being mentioned in the colophon.   There can be no doubt that De Castro printed the book.   The fine title-page, printed in red and black, with a large cut of a mounted Knight with a sword, has two of his devices in the top corners (Fig. 228).

It is a well-printed folio volume, but with the exception of the title-page and a few woodcut capitals, the decoration does not call for any special comment.   Of the rarity of the edition there can be no doubt, because the copy formerly in the Library of the Prince Marc-Antoine Borghesi, and now in the writer's collection, is the only one of which any record exists.

On the 20th November, 1547, a book appeared, " a costa de Diego Lopez librero vezino de Toledo."   It is entitled, *Tragedia Policiana.   En la qual se tractan los muy desdichados amores de Poli = /ciano y Philomena Exe/cutados por industria/de la diabolica/vieja Clau/dina, /Madre de Parme/no y maestra de Celestina.*

[1] Pérez Pastor, *La Imprenta en Medina del Campo*, Madrid, 1895 (pp. 36-37).

FIG. 228.—*Amadis de Gaula*, Medina del Campo, Juan de Villaquiran y Pedro de Castro, 1545.
(Original printed in red and black.)

Quarto in size, in Gothic type, it has thirty-five lines to a full-page and consists of seventy-seven leaves. The foliation is irregular, ending with fol. lxxx, but as the verso of the title is marked " fol. ii," and there are other mistakes, it is probable that the book contained seventy-eight leaves and that there was a blank leaf in the first signature (a4, b-k8, i2). Pérez Pastor includes this book in his bibliography of books printed at Toledo and Barrera,[1] and other writers make the same mistake, being misled by the statement in the colophon that the book was produced by " Diego Lopez, bookseller and native of Toledo." In addition, there is the further excuse that there was in fact a second edition of the play printed at Toledo the following year (1548) " en casa de Fernandez de Santa Cathalina." However, a glance at the title-page of this first edition (Fig. 229) will show that the top compartment border, signed with the initials of Juán de Vingles, as well as the inner one, are borders which Pedro de Castro habitually used in his books, and to make the matter conclusive, one of his well-known devices appears in the lower compartment border at the foot of the page. Some of the woodcut initials in the book also appear in the acknowledged productions of this printer at Medina del Campo. The title-page contains a small cut in which a young gentleman is shown presenting a flower to his lady, and twenty-nine other cuts throughout the text serve to represent some of the characters in the play. An example is here reproduced (Fig. 230). A word may be added as to the play itself. A tragedy in twenty-nine acts, it is one of the early imitations of the *Celestina*. From an acrostic, which is found in some verses at the beginning of the book, we may assume the author to have been " El Bacheller Sebastian Fernandez," and this assumption need not seriously be disturbed by a statement in the Toledo second edition of 1548, which suggests that the credit of authorship should be given to Luis

---

[1] Barrera, *Catálogo del Teatro Antiguo Español*, Madrid, 1860.

FIG. 229.—*Tragedia Policiana* [Medina del Campo, Pedro de Castro], 1547.

Hurtado.   Dr. H. Thomas has already disposed of the claims of this Luis Hurtado to have been the author of the *Palmerin de Inglaterra*, printed in Toledo in the same year and at the same press, by showing first of all, that Hurtado had really made no claim to the actual authorship, and that in the second place, that if he had written it, he must have done so at the age of fifteen, which is negatived by every consideration of reason or probability. Similarly, we may even more readily dismiss his claims to the authorship of this play.   The story of the play is as indecent as the *Celestina*, of which it is so obvious an imitation.   The lady

FIG. 230.—*Tragedia Policiana* [Medina del Campo, Pedro de Castro], 1547.

perishes at the end from the attentions of a lion, and by a testamentary document she is made to leave the secret of her magic to Celestina !   An important book in the history of the Spanish drama, the only recorded copies of the first edition being in the Biblioteca Nacional at Madrid and the Royal Library at Munich. The writer's copy was formerly in the Royal Library of Elizabeth-Farnesi, wife of Philip V., and the old calf binding has been impressed with her Arms in gold on each cover.

The last book of Pedro de Castro to which we would call attention is his *Salustio Cathilinario y Jugurta.   Cō glosa en romance*, which, on the 21st August, 1548, " Con mucha diligencia/Impresso en Medina del Cā/(*po*) por Pedro de Castro/Impressor. a costa/de Juan de Espinosa mercader de libros." It is the first Spanish edition of this translation of Videl de Noya. The title, printed in red and black, has the usual top compartment border designed by Juan de Vingles, while some of the small initial letters employed in the text are to be found in nearly all his books.   A large woodcut capital L is here reproduced (Fig. 231), as it bears the initials of the printer, P.C., and is not one I have found in any of his other books.

There is no necessity to dwell at any length on any of the other printers at this town.   On the death of Pedro de Castro,

Fig. 231.—*Salustio*, Medina del Campo, Pedro de Castro, 1548.

Diego Fernandez de Cordova, whose work we have already noticed at Valladolid, came to this town and produced a few books in which he used a decorative and pleasing device,[1] but which are otherwise unimportant.

Guillermo de Millis was primarily a bookseller and publisher, and it is only on the death of De Castro that we find him engaged as an actual printer with a press of his own.   He had been the financial backer, not only of Pedro de Castro, but also of Pierres Tobans at Salamanca, and we find his device, as well as their own, in several of their books.   As an example of his own work as a printer, we will take the *Primera y Segunda Parte*

[1] For a reproduction of this device, see Pérez Pastor, *La Imprenta en Medina del Campo*, Madrid, 1895 (p. 70).

de la Historia General de las Indias . . . con la conquista de Mexico y de la nueva España, which he printed in 1553. The book is well decorated, and the title-page of the *Conquista de Mexico*, here reproduced (Fig. 232), is a dignified piece of work.

Conquiſta de Mexico.

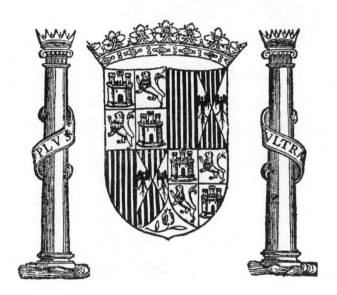

SECVNDA PARTE DELA
Chronica general delas Indias,que trata de
la conquiſta de Mexico. Nueuamente y con licencia impreſſa.
Año de. 1 5 5 3.

FIG. 232.—Lopez de Gomara—*Conquista de Mexico*, Medina del Campo, G. de Millis,
1553.
(Reduced, original 220 × 158 mm.)

A weird cut of a "vaca corcobada" (a cow with a hump, i.e. a bison!), appears in the first part of the book (Fig. 233), and must have given the readers an unnecessary scare as to the animal life to be encountered in the New World! This is the second edition of Lopez de Gomara's great historical work, which is indispensable to the student of Spanish affairs in

Mexico after the conquest.   One may here quote some remarkable words from the author's dedication to Charles V. :
"The greatest event which has happened since the creation of
the world (leaving aside the incarnation and death of Him
who created it) is the discovery of the Indies."   The book is
rarely found in good condition and copies are scarce.   These

FIG. 233.—Lopez de Gomara—*Conquista de Mexico*, Medina del Campo, G. de Millis, 1553.

reproductions have been made from a copy formerly in the
collection of Lord Stuart de Rothesay, Ambassador at Madrid
and Lisbon, which bears his Arms on the covers.

Vincente de Millis, a son of Guillermo, followed in the
parental footsteps.   I am able to give as an example of his
work, an extremely rare piece which he printed in 1572, entitled, *Relacion verdadera de lo sucedido en Chypre en la qual se
cuenta como ciertos captivos Christianos se levantaron con la galera*

capitana del Turco.   The cut on the title-page, which is presumably meant to represent Famagosta in Cyprus, is here reproduced (Fig. 234).   This contemporary news-sheet tells the story of the capture of Cyprus by the Turks from the Republic of Venice in 1571-72.   The investment of the seaport of Famagosta is described, and an interesting story is told of the capture by some

FIG. 234.—*Relacion verdadera de lo sucedido en Chypre,* Medina del Campo, Vincente de Millis, 1572.

Christian prisoners, assisted by a renegade Spaniard, of a Turkish flag-ship, which they succeeded in carrying off to Candia, together with an account of their further adventures at Mecina and Palermo.   This fugitive and ephemeral production, of which I can find no record, was discovered in the binding of a book formerly in the Royal Library of Carlos I., King of Portugal.

CHAPTER XVII.

SEGOVIA, CUENCA, ASTORGA AND MADRID.

JUAN DE LA CUESTA, who was afterwards to obtain enduring
fame as the printer at Madrid who produced the first edition of
Don Quixote, was the chief printer in Segovia in the sixteenth
century.

Of his illustrated books, we may mention the *Emblemas
Morales* of Juan Horozco y Covaruvias, which, according to the
colophon, was printed in 1589, but which bears the date of
1591 upon the title-page. The text contains about one hundred
large cuts illustrating the emblems. These occupy most of the
page and are within architectural borders, with the text of each
emblem in the centre. These cuts are of little or no artistic
merit, and they are not improved by being printed, if my copy
of the first edition is a fair sample, upon exceedingly poor paper.

This book of emblems is a book that habitually turns up
in the sale rooms and enjoys the attention of booksellers and
collectors to a larger extent than, in my opinion, its intrinsic
merits deserve.

CUENCA.

Franciscus de Alfaro, who printed two books at Toledo,
seems to have printed three in this town, of which one, the
Meditationes Jordani de vida et passione Christi (see Heredia Sale
Catalogue, No. 4008), printed in 1530-31, has a number of
cuts of the ordinary type associated with a book of this kind.
The productions of the other printers in this town, during the
century, are similarly without interest from our point of view.

ASTORGA

Two printers paid short visits to this town, Augustin de Paz in 1547, and Pedro Cosin thirty years later. Augustin de Paz had worked at Zamora, Mondoñedo and Oviedo, and is recorded in these towns by Gutiérrez del Caño in his most useful list of Spanish printers,[1] but he was apparently unaware that he had worked at Astorga, and starts the press in this town with Pedro Cosin in 1577. A discovery I have made of three tracts of Savonarola, which were printed by Augustin de Paz here in 1547, and two other books of the same year, which are in the British Museum, fix the correct date of the establishment of a printing press in the town. The titles and colophons of these tracts are :—

(a) *Exposicion del psalmo de Misrere mei*, " Astorga en casa de/Augustin de Paz. Acabo/se a. xxii. del mes de/Marco./ M.D.XLVII./ "

(b) *Exposicion del psalmo de Qui regis israel*, " Astorga en casa de/Augustin de Paz. Acabo/se a. xxviii del mes de/Marco/ M.D.XLVII./ "

(c) *Exposicion del psalmo. In te domine speravi*, " Astorga en casa de/Augustin de Paz. Acabo/se a. xxxi. del mes de/Marco/ M.D.XLVII./ "

These tracts are in quarto, and each of them was separately printed with a decorative woodcut title-page, with a cut of King David within borders. It will be seen from the reproduction of one of them (Fig. 235) that the cut has plenty of detail and is signed with a small monogram, apparently made up of the initials of the printer.

MADRID.

For its size and importance, this is a most disappointing town as far as our particular subject is concerned. In the first

[1] Marcelino Gutiérrez del Caño, *Ensayo de un Catálogo de Impresores Españoles desde la introduccion de la Imprenta hasta fines del siglo XVIII*. (Articles in the " Revista de Archivos, Bibliotecas y Museos," Madrid, 1899-1900.)

FIG. 235.—Savonarola—*Exposicion sobre el psalmo de Miserere mei*, Astorga, Augustin de Paz, 1547.

place, no press was established in Madrid until 1566, which is
of course a much later date than any of the other big Spanish
towns. The definite choice of the City in 1561 as the residence
of the King and the Court, was no doubt responsible for the
establishment of a printing press, and the only wonder is that
five years elapsed before Alonso Gomez, in conjunction with
Pierres Cosin, issued the first production from their press. The
partnership does not appear to have lasted long, as in 1568 we
find that they had parted company and each had his own
separate establishment. If we except a book like the *Tractado
breve y compendioso sobre la máravillosa obra de la boca y dentadura*
of Francisco Martinez de Castrillo, printed by Alonso Gomez in
1570, which has some cuts interspersed in the text, the writing
books of Francisco Lucus, or some cuts of Antonio Arfe, none
of which are of great interest or importance, we find that the
record of the printing press at Madrid during the first two
decades of its existence, and for all practical purposes up to the
end of the century, is one which is singularly free from any
attempt to provide the reading public with books, in which
either decoration or illustration formed any conspicuous feature.
One reason for this is to be found in the very large output of
official publications during the period in question, a class of
literature, which then, as now, did not lend itself to much, if
any, artistic treatment. We must therefore content ourselves
with the available material and give one or two examples of the
book decoration and illustration at Madrid during the last years
of the sixteenth century, which may fairly be taken as a reasonable sample of the whole.

As a specimen of the official class of publication, let us take
a *Pragmatica y Declaracion sobre los que permiten que sus mugeres
sean malas, seles da la pena que a los Rufianes*, issued by Philip II.
in February, 1575, and printed by Alonso Gomez in that year
(Fig. 236). A simple and well-arranged title-page, entirely
adequate for the subject of a Royal Ordinance directed against

husbands, who, for a money consideration, allow their wives to misconduct themselves with other men. It is of interest to note that the penalty prescribed for a second offence was one hundred lashes and perpetual imprisonment in the Galleys! In this

PRAGMATICA Y DE-
claracion fobre los que permiten que
fus mugeres fean malas, feles da la
pena que a los Rufianes.

En Madrid en cafa de Alonfo Gomez,
Imprefsor de fu Mageftad. Año
1 5 7 5.

Efta taffado en quatro marauedis.

FIG. 236.—*Pragmatica*, Madrid, Alonso Gomez, 1575.
(Reduced, original 235 × 125 mm.)

matter at any rate, the morality of his subjects seems to have been adequately conserved by Philip, so far as the deterrent nature of the punishment is concerned. Another, and a later example of this kind of publication, is to be found in the extremely rare and historically important Account of the Spanish Armada, which

Philip II. ordered to be printed in 1588. It bears the following title : *Relacion verdadera del Armada, que el Rey Don Felippe nuestro señor mando juntar en el puerto de la Cidad de Lisbon en el Reyno de Portugal el año de* 1588. It was printed by the

RELACION VERDA
dera del Armada, que el Rey Don Felippe
nueſtro ſeñor mando juntar en el puerto de
la cidad de Lisboa en el Reyno
de Portugal el año de
1588.

Que començo a ſalir del Puerto a los veynte y nueue de Mayo,
y acabo de ſalir a los treynta, y ſe hizo a la vela, que
nueſtro Señor la encamine en ſu
ſanto ſeruicio.

CON LICENCIA
EN MADRID
Por la viuda de Alonſo Gomez Impreſſor del
Rey nueſtro ſeñor.
Vendeſe en caſa de Blas de Robles librero del Rey nueſtro ſeñor

FIG. 237.—*Relacion verdadera del Armada*, Madrid, viuda de Alonso Gomez, 1588.
(Reduced, original 242 × 143 mm.)

widow of Alonso Gomez at Madrid in 1588. Here again the decoration of the title-page (Fig. 237) is very simple, and one would have at least expected a representation of one of the invincible galleons of which so much was hoped. The rarity of this official and contemporary Spanish Account of the Armada, of which the only recorded copy (other than the one in my collection) is in the Library of the Royal Academy of History at Madrid, is perhaps sufficient excuse for giving some brief particulars of its contents. In a more detailed title, which appears on the second leaf, we are told that this is an Account of the number of ships (their classes being detailed) which were assembled in the River of Lisbon, "whereof is Chief and General, the Duke of Medina Sidonia. Together with their burden, the men of war, mariners, munitions, weapons, artillery, powder, and other furnitures for war, which they bring and for what period they serve." Minute details are given of the tonnage of each ship, its cargo of arms and munitions, the officers, naval and military (with their names and rank) on board. Particulars are also given of the standards and banners, on which are painted portraits of Jesus Christ, Our Lady and the Royal Arms of Spain. An interesting point in connexion with this publication is the fact that in 1588 John Wolfe printed in London *A True Discourse of the Armada* which was stated to have been "translated out of the French into English by Daniel Archdeacon." There is a Preface to this signed by E.B., in which all the vituperative resources of the Old Testament are invoked against Philip, who is compared to Sennacherib! With the exception of this Preface, the English version is a more or less literal translation of this Spanish one. If it was translated from the French, that in turn must have been made from this Spanish original. It is possible that E.B. was Edward Banister, who induced Bartholomew Young to make his translation of Montemayor's *Diana*. Banister was himself a student of Spanish and in close association with the English Catholic refugees in Spain.

A chance discovery of the writer, while turning over a bundle of fugitive tracts in the shop of a Barcelona bookseller, resulted in the acquisition of this contemporary Spanish publication, of such profound interest to all Englishmen.

Mention may be made of another book produced by the

widow of Alonso Gomez in the following year (1589).   It is
of an entirely different character, being the *Primera Parte de
las Elegias de Varones illustres de Indias* of Juan de Castellanos.
The book is of considerable American interest, consisting as it
does of the lives (in verse) of some of the early discoverers and
adventurers in the New World.   It is in quarto, and on the
verso of the seventh leaf, there is a full-page cut containing the
Arms of Philip II., and beneath them an allegorical figure of
" Hispania," who is depicted carrying the blessings of religion
and civilisation to the newly-discovered lands.   The whole is
surrounded by tropical foliage and vegetation, birds of varied
plumage, leopards and monkeys (179 × 126 mm.).   There is
also in the book a full-page woodcut portrait of the author,
which Salvá has reproduced (vol. i., p. 202).

Pedro Madrigal, one of the most famous printers in Madrid
at this period, was responsible for a large output of books in all
classes of literature, from 1577 and onwards for a period which
extended into the opening years of the seventeenth century.   An
example of his work is to be found in the *Comentarios de Don
Bernardino de Mendoça, de lo sucedido en las Guerras de los Payses
baxos, desde el Año de 1567 hasta el de 1577*, which he printed
in 1592.   The title-page bears his extremely pretty device
(Fig. 238).   It is the same one used later on by Juan del a Cuesta
on the title-page of the first edition of *Don Quixote* in 1605.
Madrigal has employed here a copper plate for the design, instead of the usual woodcut.   The book has also another copper-
plate engraving which illustrates a contrivance used during the
wars in the Low Countries to obstruct the enemy's cavalry.

Tomas Junti was appointed King's Printer in 1594.   In
that year he published the *De confirmando Concilio Illiberritano*
of Fernando Mendoza, which is a handsome folio volume in
which copper-plate work is employed, not only for illustrating
the text, but also for the title-page (Fig. 239).   The copy of this
book from which this reproduction is made is of special associa-

tion interest. Bound in old Spanish brown calf, with gilt-line tooling on the covers, it bears the Arms in gold on each of them of Philip II. It is a duplicate from the Library of the Escorial, and a signed statement to this effect by Fr. Lucas de Alaejos, Keeper of the books at the Escorial, appears on the flyleaf (Fig. 240). He certifies under date 1613, that the book was a duplicate and had been sold by permission of the King and of

FIG. 238.—Mendoza—*Comentarios*, Madrid, Pedro Madrigal, 1592. (Device of printer.)

the Convent. Later on, the book passed into the possession of the shod (as opposed to the barefooted) Order of Carmelites. This work of Mendoza was placed upon the *Index librorum prohibitorum* in 1612, and under a date in July, 1613, there is a certificate that it has been altered in accordance with the requirements of the Holy Office, by the deletion of some lines on page 92 of Bk. II. of the volume, and on referring to the passage in this copy, the objectionable words are to be found pasted over with a strip of paper !   The Carmelites, when they got the book, had it certified as conforming to the requirements of a later

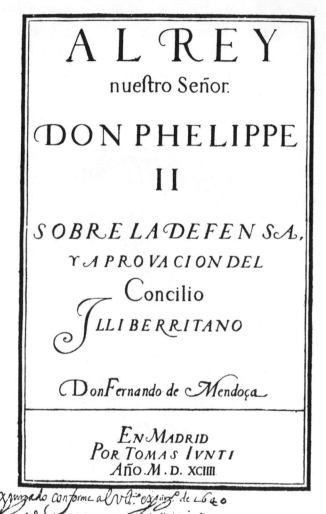

FIG. 239.—Fernando de Mendoça—*De confirmando Concilio Illiberitano*, Madrid, Tomas Junti, 1594.
(Reduced, original 249 × 153 mm.)

Index of 1640, and this certificate bears the autograph of Dionysius Jubero " calificador " (i.e. Examiner of books and writings) of the Sacred Office of the Inquisition. The book has the press mark of the Escorial Library written on the fore-edge, as all the books in the cases of that Library had, and still have, their edges, instead of their backs, turned to the spectator, a system initiated by Arias Montano, the first Librarian. The book itself deals with the Council of Illiberri (Elvira), which took place A.D. 324. The decrees of this Council were all through the centuries a matter of contention. Philip II., who was a supporter of them, commissioned Mendoza, a learned jurist, to write this defence, with the object of sending it to Rome for propaganda purposes. The issue was in consequence a very limited one and copies are scarce.

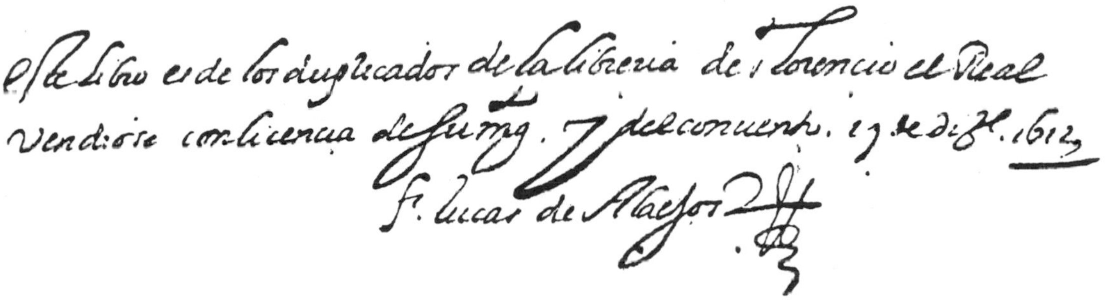

FIG. 240.—Inscription in the copy of Mendoça's *De confirmando Concilio Illiberitano*, Madrid, 1594.

We will conclude our consideration of the Madrid printers by referring to Luis Sanchez, who was at work for the long period of sixty-three years.

We will take as an example of his press a book that will always live in the history of Spanish literature, the *Arcadia, Prosas y Versos* of the world-famous dramatist, Lope de Vega. Pérez Pastor, in his "Bibliografía Madrileña" (Madrid, 1891), under the year 1598, enters, on the authority of Ticknor, a single line entry, without any particulars, of this book. He goes on to say that the majority of bibliographers believe that the first edition of the *Arcadia* was not published until 1599. In his opinion, the fact that the "tasa," or license to print, in the 1599 edition was dated in that year, is strong evidence that the book then appeared for the first time, because printers, when they contemplated a second edition of a book, usually abstained from applying for a second "tasa," and inserted the previous one with

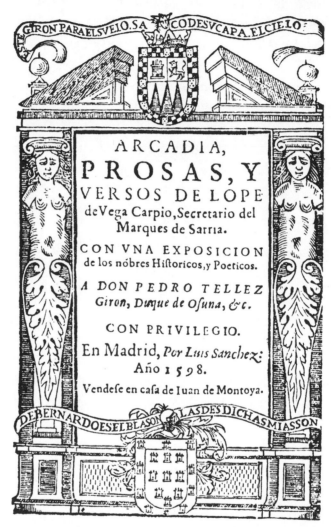

FIG. 241.—Lope de Vega—*Arcadia*, Madrid, Luis Sanchez, 1598.

the original date, in order to avoid the burden of supplying copies to each member of the Council, and to the Library of the Escorial, which involved a gratuitous distribution of some twenty-seven copies of the book. It would seem to have been a more exacting requirement than even under our copyright laws to-day. Under these circumstances, Pastor thinks that if there had been an edition of 1598, that the second edition would have had its "tasa" dated in that year and not 1599. The discovery of a copy of the actual edition of 1598 enables us

QVIDHVMILITATEJNVIDIA?

FIG. 242.—Lope de Vega—*Arcadia*, Madrid, Luis Sanchez, 1598.

to set the matter finally at rest. It is an octavo volume, and corresponds in all material particulars with the edition of 1599 (Pastor, No. 663), but the "tasa" is dated the 27th of November, 1598, which year also appears clearly on the title-page, which is here reproduced (Fig. 241). The book is well printed, and in addition to the decorative title-page, has a good cut of the Giron

Arms on the last leaf of the text.   Moreover, Sanchez provides the readers of the book with a woodcut portrait of the author. This is found on the verso of fol. 8 facing the first page of the text (Fig. 242).   The portrait shows Lope de Vega as a young man, in what appears to be military uniform.   At the foot is the motto " Quid humilitate invidia," and the cut is signed I.S.D., the last letter being somewhat indistinct.   This portrait is found again in the 1599 edition, but is entirely different to the one appearing in later Madrid editions (e.g. the one of 1603), and in the *Hermosura de Angelica* of 1602, or to the one in *Jerusalen conquistada* of 1609, which portrait Francisco Pachecho seems to have copied, as far as the head only is concerned, from the portrait in this 1598 *Arcadia*.

With these notes on the decoration and illustration of a book, which Ticknor assumes, and I think rightly, to be the first work published by Lope de Vega, we can fittingly conclude our consideration of Madrid book decoration and illustration in the sixteenth century, which quite obviously was of a very slight and unimportant character.

CHAPTER XVIII.

ANTEQUERA, BILBAO AND MALAGA.

THE small town of Antequera is of some typographical note owing to the press that was established there " In aedibus Ælii Nebrissensis" for the production of some of the works of the famous grammarian and man of letters, Antonius Ælius Nebrissensis. We have already seen that his son, Sancho de Lebrija, had a press at Granada from 1533 to 1552, and it is not unlikely that he was responsible for this branch establishment at a neighbouring town. As an example of restrained and simple title decoration, we can take the *Sapientum Dicta Vafre et Acutissime cum Glosemate*, which was printed here in 1577 (Fig. 243). In passing from this place we can do no better than reproduce the striking woodcut portrait of Nebrissensis, which appears on the title-page of his *Dictionarium*, printed in the town in 1581 (Fig. 244).

BILBAO.

Matías Marés was the chief sixteenth-century printer at Bilbao, and books from his press are so rare, that it is difficult to give any exact particulars of the proportion of them that deserve any notice from our point of view. I have one book from his press, which in all probability is a fair sample of his work. It is *Los Colloquios Satiricos con un colloquio pastoril*, by Antonio de Torquemada, which he printed in this town in 1584. A little octavo volume, its decoration is quite up to the average of the period. Some interesting woodcut capitals, including one representing a woman in the stocks (Fig. 245), and the Arms of the City on the last leaf (Fig. 246), are not without interest. Marés had previously printed at Salamanca, and when he left Bilbao, he started a press at Logroño in 1588.

Of other books at Bilbao, *Las Prematicas, ordenancas, ley, y folcutad dada por sus Magestades, por Privilegio especial, a la uni-*

**SAPIENTVM DI-
CTA VAFRE ET ACVTIS-
SIME CVM GLOSEMATE**
Aelij Antonij Nebriſſenſis
*nunc denuo recognita &
emendata.*

ANTIQVARIAE.
In ædibus Aelij Antonij Nebriſſenſis.
Anno 1577.

FIG. 243.—Nebrissensis—*Sapientum Dicta Vafre*, Antequera, 1577.

versidad de la contratacion de los fiel, y Consules de la muy noble villa de Bilbao, a folio volume, printed by " Iuan de lorza, Impressor del muy Noble, y muy Leal Senorio de Vizcaia," which unfortunately bears no date, but the introduction to which is dated 1552, seems quite possibly to have been printed in the sixteenth

FIG. 244.—Nebrissensis—*Dictionarium*, Antequera, 1581.

FIG. 245.—Antonio de Torquemada—*Los Colloquios Satiricos*, Bilbao, Matias Mares, 1584.

century. It has a quaint cut of a ship on the title (Fig. 247), which we find again in a similar work which was published well on in the seventeenth century, but in which the block had much deteriorated by wear.

MALAGA.

In this town, Juan René was the only sixteenth-century printer. His first book at this press was the *Segunda Parte y*

FIG. 246.—Antonio Torquemada—*Los Colloquios Satiricos*, Bilbao, Matias Mares, 1584.

libro septimo de la Descripcion General de Africa of Luys de la Marmol Caravajal, which was printed in 1599. It has a good cut of the Royal Arms on the title, some crude woodcut capitals which had obviously seen much service elsewhere, and a full-page cut of Arms on the last page,[1] which also does duty as the device of Rene Rabut, the Granada printer, who had printed the first volume of this work at that town in 1573.

[1] For reproduction, see Haebler, *Spanische und Portugiesische Bucherzeichen*, Strassburg, 1898 (Tafel xxxii).

LAS PREMATICAS,
ordenanças, ley, y falcutad dada por sus
Mageſtades, por Priuilegio eſpecial, ala
vmiuerſidad de la contratacion de los
fiel, y Conſules de la muy noble
villa de Bilbao.

FIG. 247.—*Las Prematicas*, Bilbao, Juan de Lorza, *c.* 1552.
(Reduced, original 214 × 161 mm.)

CHAPTER XIX.

CONCLUSION.

In bringing to an end this partial and necessarily inadequate outline of early illustrated Spanish books, there are certain broad conclusions which may be drawn from the available material which has been at our disposal.

In the first place, a tribute should be paid to the energy and enterprise which characterised the early printers of Spain, whether immigrants from Germany or native-born masters of the craft. They lost no time, as a rule, in producing their literary wares in the vernacular. Their press work was careful and their types clear and well designed. Their decoration and illustrations were imposing from their very simplicity, while very seldom does one find in a Spanish incunable cuts which have no possible connexion with the contents of the book, a practice not so uncommon in the early history of book illustration in other countries. Above all, they impressed upon their work a national character and atmosphere, which enables the student of early typography to identify, without much difficulty, a specimen of early Spanish printing when place and printer have been omitted. If their illustrations lacked some of the special artistic merit which is found in the early illustrated books of Italy and France, it is, I suggest, only because they placed more importance upon the strong and effective decoration and illustration of the printed page than upon the production of illustrated works of art in which the contents of the book and the message it was intended to convey took a secondary place.

My friend, Mr. Updike, who has laid all students of early typography under such deep obligation by his wonderful survey of the history of printing types,[1] confesses that it is difficult to define what we all recognise as the essentially " Spanish " nature of the early printing in the Peninsula.   I can only suggest that an illustrated fifteenth-century Spanish book is notable, in comparison with other countries, for an austere magnificence, which was also to be found in other departments of Spanish life and character.   Spanish art was often sombre, and nearly always imposing, and this is not surprising in a country in which religion was so dominating and impelling a factor.   Spain had no place in her scheme of things for the trifling or the merely ornate.   Artistic refinements were always less to the Spaniard than the expression of a virile and vigorous outlook upon men and things.   We find this reflected in her fifteenth-century book illustration.   This is not perhaps very original in treatment, but when she did borrow, it was the bold and the masculine that attracted her, and her adaptations were always on these lines.   The handsome, well-adjusted title-page of a Spanish early printed book will bear comparison with those of any other country in Europe.   It is very much to be regretted that surviving examples are so scarce, more especially here in England.

In book decoration and illustration, true greatness is only achieved when the decoration and illustration blend with the letterpress to form one harmonious whole.   Judged by this standard, Spanish books in the fifteenth century occupy a very high if not a commanding position, a position to some extent maintained in the succeeding century, but one which was destined to suffer at least partial eclipse in the centuries that have followed.

When we leave the fifteenth century, and attempt to review the work of the succeeding one, our task becomes much more

---

[1] Daniel Berkeley Updike, *Printing Types, their History, Forms and Use, A Study in Survivals*, Harvard University Press, 1922.

difficult. The number of printers increased enormously, and in consequence, the field is almost limitless in its dimensions. Speaking broadly, the work of the first half of the century was vastly superior to that of the second half, which is a characteristic of most other countries besides Spain. Competition did not, as a rule, produce better and more artistic work. In the early days, the illuminated manuscript was a serious rival and put the early printers upon their mettle to produce something which would bear comparison with the work of the scribes and illuminators. As years went on, this incentive became of less importance. Decoration and illustration, and in many cases, the actual printing, deteriorated to an alarming extent, with the result that we have seen in the comparative poor work from say 1575 to the end of the century. I think it must be admitted that this is not true of the first half, when the work done, will, in its own way, especially as regards the decoration of the printed page, compare favourably with any other country in Europe. The work at Barcelona, Valencia, Zaragoza and Seville, for example, is of a very high quality, and specially is this so in the case of the Catalan towns. One has, however, always the uneasy feeling that if anything like the amount of painstaking research had been devoted to other parts of Spain, as has been so lavishly employed by the Catalan literary and bibliographical enthusiasts, we might have had material available which would have modified our views. In the absence of any such evidence, we can only conclude that there was in fact an earlier, and more sustained superiority of native workmanship and artistic effort in say Barcelona, than in almost any other town in the Peninsula. I am not unmindful of the good work produced by Coci at Zaragoza and the Crombergers at Seville, but from the point of view of the general average of original work, I incline to place Barcelona and a town like Valencia, ahead of them. It must, however, be clearly realised that the material available upon which adequate and definite conclusions can be based does not exist to-day. It will not do so, unless and until the libraries of the various Religious Houses, and those in private hands, yield up their secrets to a greater extent than has hitherto been the case. In the pages of this book, one has only to note the number of books which have hitherto been unrecorded, and apparently exist in single copies, to realise how many more remain to be discovered, and which some day will make their appearance, confounding some, if not all, of our preconceived conclusions. However, the information we do have at our disposal, and a perusal of the reproductions in the previous chapters, are sufficient to indicate that book illustration in Spain in the fifteenth century and the decoration of the books in the succeeding one, present features of considerable interest, show some artistic merit, and above all, are remarkably national in character and atmosphere. In these respects, superior to the output, for example, in our own country during the same period. In England, there is little or nothing left for the bibliographer to discover. In Spain, the soil upon the top has, up to the present, been only very indifferently disturbed. If this attempted contribution to the process leads to further and better exploratory work, the object of the present writer will have been more than fulfilled.

FINIS.

INDEX.

The following are grouped together:—AUTHORS (and anonymous works);
DEVICES OF PRINTERS; ENGRAVERS' INITIALS; OWNERS; PRINTERS
(with towns).